GW00645731

My Passport Says Clairvoyant

MY PASSPORT SAYS CLAIRVOYANT

M. B. Dykshoorn

as told to

Russell H. Felton

HAWTHORN BOOKS, INC.

Publishers/New York

MY PASSPORT SAYS CLAIRVOYANT

Copyright © 1974 by M. B. Dykshoorn and Russell H. Felton. Copyright under International and Pan-American Copyright Conventions. All rights reserved, including the right to reproduce this book or portions thereof in any form, except for the inclusion of brief quotations in a review. All inquiries should be addressed to Hawthorn Books, Inc., 260 Madison Avenue, New York, New York 10016. This book was manufactured in the United States of America and published simultaneously in Canada by Prentice-Hall of Canada, Limited, 1870 Birchmount Road, Scarborough, Ontario.

Library of Congress Catalog Card Number: 74-2579

ISBN: 0-8015-5282-6

First Printing, October 1974
Second Printing, November 1974

For Cora,
with love and gratitude
from both of us

CONTENTS

My Passport Says Clairvoyant

PROLOGUE

Investigation in Appalachia

Early in 1972, on a bitterly cold and blustery yet dry and snowless day at the tail end of winter, a project that had already consumed my time and enthusiasm for three years on three continents took me high into the Appalachian Mountains of the southern United States in the company of two men I had come to know well.

One, our driver, was Charlotte, North Carolina, businessman James G. Bolton, a slow-talking native Carolinian with a quick, inquisitive intelligence, a legalistic turn of mind, and a bent for meticulous observation. He had left his real estate business to run itself for the day and come along, I knew, to indulge a passionate enthusiasm: to observe, witness, record, and document in minute detail any "unusual" events that might take place that day.

And both Jim Bolton and I knew there was a strong likelihood that events would take place that would need to be witnessed and documented.

Jim knew because he had gone along before with our companion, on other days like this one, to other towns and cities, to observe, witness, and document.

I knew because I had spent years in other places—in Europe, Australia, and America—verifying reports from witnesses of other "unusual" events, the like of which we were expecting. Strange, improbable, almost fantastic events, spanning a quarter of a century: human bodies uncovered from canals and rivers, or exhumed from ancient, unmarked graves; vital leads given to police in cases of disappearance and even murder; criminal cases solved over international long-distance telephone lines; caches of money, ancient relics, buildings, ships, and even animals found by one man using no identifiable method, yet apparently with the ease of a librarian selecting books from a shelf.

All these cases and dozens, even hundreds more, had come supported by documented evidence, much of it legally admissible and virtually all of it readily verifiable. And it all pointed to one barely credible conclusion: that our companion, the third man in our car, had somehow *caused* all these things to happen.

For our companion was no ordinary man, and his mission was no ordinary mission, that day in the mountains.

He was a clairvoyant—a "psychic"—and not only *a* psychic, but perhaps the most gifted, and certainly the most accomplished, psychic of our time or perhaps of any time. His record, to quote from a French newspaper report of one of his most spectacular cases, was "long and beyond dispute." He was the only psychically gifted person ever to have been recognized by the government of any country: The government of his native Netherlands had issued him a passport listing his occupation unequivocally as *helderziende* —"clairvoyant."

And today he was going into the mountains to test his abilities on yet another case. He was going to conduct a "psychic investigation" of an unsolved case of murder.

We arrived in the small mountain town shortly after nine in the morning and were met by the sheriff, a deputy, and the local chief of police. The sheriff was a mountain himself, easily six-four and 280 pounds, a man as tough and rugged as the hills he policed. Leading us into a small back room, he gave the impression he could cross the room from door to window in a single, huge stride.

At this point we—the clairvoyant, Jim Bolton, and I—knew

nothing more about the case than we had read in the newspapers. Some months before, the bodies of four people had been found in a house on the outskirts of town. They had been strangled. This was all we knew, except that after months of investigation the police had made no arrests. Finally the sheriff had quietly sought the assistance of the clairvoyant, who had already worked on five similar cases in the South, with remarkable results.

He had worked on these cases, as he was working on this one, without publicity and without financial reward. News of his involvement had been carefully kept out of the press, and this was the way he liked it. In fact, he insisted upon it. But the value of his work for law enforcement agencies in the South could be measured by the quiet recognition he had received.

Twice he had been made an associate member of the Sheriff's Association of North Carolina, and in May of 1971 the then governor of Kentucky, Louis B. Nunn, had commissioned him a Kentucky colonel "in consideration of outstanding achievement." At that time he had been living in the United States for a little more than a year.

In the back room the sheriff began explaining the circumstances of the case, but to his surprise the clairvoyant cut him short.

"Please," he said, "tell me nothing about the case. Let me work it out for myself."

The sheriff looked taken aback, but he shrugged. "All right, fine," he said. "They tell me you have your own way, so you just go ahead. Just tell us what you want."

"I need to visit the house," the clairvoyant told him. "I'm sorry, but it is better that you tell me nothing about the case. I will try to work it out and later you can ask me questions. But now I would like to visit the house."

The sheriff and deputy drove us to the house in which the bodies had been found several months earlier—and there began the most phenomenal series of events I had ever witnessed.

The house, halfway up a scarred and broken-grounded hillside, had been emptied of furniture and placed under lock and key since the murders. Its modern, cheerful exterior belied the savagery that had manifested itself within the walls. It was hard to believe that inside this house four innocent people had been killed.

The sheriff let us in with a key—and things began happening with bewildering speed. The clairvoyant drew from his jacket pocket a length of thin wire bent into a loop, and gripping it in both hands, loop extended in front, he started pacing from room to empty room. The loop of wire spun frantically in his hands. It did not appear that the clairvoyant was making it spin; it seemed to spin of its own accord.

The clairvoyant moved from room to room busily, quickly, frowning over the spinning wire, pausing, hesitating, seeming to step around objects invisible to the rest of us. Suddenly, after stepping into the living room, he halted. Then he lurched, stumbled, bent double, fell to his knees, gagging as though something had caught in his throat, coughing, choking, and gasping for breath. The veins leaped out of his neck and blood rushed to his face. His eyes bulged and his hands grasped at his throat. But just as the officers and I rushed to support him he straightened again as abruptly as he had slumped, and the face he turned on us was impassive, undistressed, even apologetic.

"It's all right," he said. "I'm sorry, I'm all right now."

He looked so composed, and so shortly after his paroxysm of distress, that we were pulled up short in our rush to help him. The compulsive spasm seemed to have passed over him like a breath of cold wind.

For a while he stood still, frowning again over the strange loop of wire in his hands, then he strode into another room as though nothing had happened, leaving the rest of us staring after him in amazement.

But a minute later it happened again! And then again. And again. Four times the clairvoyant stumbled and fell suddenly, gagging and gasping as though struggling with some invisible assailant, choking on his own breath, and each time he recovered in an instant to carry on his erratic tour of the empty house.

Were these histrionics? Was this showmanship, or exhibitionism? The only spectators were Jim Bolton and I, both friends of his, and the two officers, both of whom seemed more disturbed than impressed by this startling development.

For my own part, I had been more or less expecting incidents of this kind. Many reliable witnesses of this man's remarkable work had reported that while concentrating on the victims of violent crimes or accidents he seemed to undergo extreme yet momentary physical distress. But this was the first time I had ever actually witnessed the phenomenon, and in spite of my anticipation of it I began to feel distinctly uneasy. Something was happening that I could not begin to comprehend, and the implications were enormous. For the clairvoyant had just gone through, in a psychic sense, the experience of being strangled—four times!

Now he returned to the living room, looking tense but composed, and in a quiet voice he told how each victim had died.

"It was so," he said. "They were killed in different rooms, then all the bodies were dragged together and put one on top of the other. That was how you found them."

It was not a question, but a statement of fact. The officers exchanged glances, but said nothing.

"Their hands were tied behind their backs," the clairvoyant said. "They were beaten, bruised on the face. The strangling was done from behind, with a knee in the back, quickly, with a curtain cord. I am sorry, but I don't think you will find it now. It is gone."

Then the clairvoyant announced the second phase of his psychic investigation. He would "follow, like a police dog," he said, the path each separate member of the killing party had taken from the house on the night of the murder, several months before.

"We will take each of them in turn," he said. "I will show you where they went."

At first the officers could barely comprehend the clairvoyant's intentions. He would concentrate, in his unique way, on each individual and unknown member of the killing party and he would lead us along the route each of them had taken in making his escape from the house. He would make all the stops along the way, register every psychic impression he received from that night months in the past, and he would lead the police right to the place where each of the killers had spent that night.

And all these things he proceeded to do.

It took all the rest of the morning and half the afternoon. The clairvoyant led us into the woods, along rough, incongruent paths, over fences, along roads and streets and highways of the town and the county which he seemed to know like the back of his hand although the rest of us knew for certain he had never before been in that locality.

Following some instinctive "guidance system," always with the loop of wire spinning tirelessly in his hands, he led us right to the doors of houses and places of business, into the driveways and parking lots of gas stations, and once to a small hotel with an improbable back-street location. Where he believed a killer had walked on the night of the murders, he walked now.

Whenever he felt that a killer had driven a car, we climbed into the police car and drove with the clairvoyant giving directions. "Turn left . . . slow down . . . now faster . . . slower, a little slower . . . turn right here . . . wait, stop. He stopped here . . . back up . . one got out here. There is another car waiting. A truck, a pick-up truck—five, six years old. Blue. It makes a lot of noise. . . ."

Throughout, the clairvoyant was in a state of deep concentration, but not in a trance. His face began to look more and more tense and haggard, more deeply lined, drawn taut by the strain of concentration sustained for hours on end.

But all the time information poured out of him in short, sharp statements. All of them were taken down verbatim by the deputy.

"There were three in the car. They stopped. Two got out. The first went on. Alone? Yes, alone. We'll follow him now, come back later for the others. . . . This hamburger place—is it open all night? I see a light inside. . . ."

It was broad daylight, but in his mind the clairvoyant had somehow gone back in time to a night months in the past. He was aware of us and of his real surroundings, but some part of his mind was in another car, and it was night.

"Slow down. Turn left. He stopped here. He was alone. The tall one. This is the killer. He went in this door. He went on? No, he stayed here. This is where he spent the night. . . ."

We were parked in the lot of a tire recapping business. A few bystanders watched us curiously. The clairvoyant was pointing directly at a doorway leading into the building. It was wide open, but he talked as if it were closed. "He had a key. He works here. He spent the night here. They know him. All these people know him. He works here in this place. His car was parked here all night. . . ."

Then we went back and "followed" the others—from the house. We moved on foot through the woods. We rode in the police car. Once the clairvoyant made us stop at a green light because the other car, the one he saw in his mind, stopped when the light was red.

Patterns began to take form: the killers' rendezvous; one abandoned a car in a parking lot, another came by to pick him up; one went to a house and remained there, others spent the dangerous night in factories or hiding places. One stopped at the all-night hamburger place and asked the waitress for change for the pay phone. She knows him personally, the clairvoyant says. She will remember having seen him that night.

Then a truly astounding thing happened—an incident which, although comparatively unremarkable against the broader history of this clairvoyant's achievements, still causes me to start in wonder as I write about it.

Once again the clairvoyant led us from the house, by way of a back route, directly to a factory in the town and through the open gate of its parking lot. The gateman peered at us in surprise and suddenly it seemed strange, even slightly ridiculous, to be following the directions of a clairvoyant whose mind was in the past while around us the world went blithely about its business.

But in an instant the mood changed. The deputy, unable to hold down his dismay, blurted out a revelation. Employed at this factory, he said, is a prime suspect in the case—a man who might have had a motive to kill. The suspect had argued with one of the victims over money. Threats had been made.

Of all the buildings in town, the clairvoyant had brought us to this one. And he had not only brought us there, but brought us by the most direct route from the house—by a shortcut, in fact, along an un-signposted back road which only local people knew led to this part of town. And the clairvoyant has never been in this county before.

Back in the sheriff's office, the clairvoyant invited the officers to ask him questions. "Ask me anything," he said. "I will try to work it out."

Ask me questions, he urged, and the officers complied. They did so hesitantly at first; lingering doubts and a natural embarrassment restrained them from full acceptance of the possibility that the clairvoyant *really* knew. How many killers were there? Are they local people, or from out of town? The clairvoyant answered positively, unambiguously, patiently.

What time did the killings take place?

"Time is difficult," he replied. "I think it was about eleven o'clock."

As additional queries were thrown out, he began to respond with more and more detail. And as the details built on one another the officers asked more daring questions, requiring precise, specific answers.

Oddly enough, the more specific the questions, the more detailed were the answers. The clairvoyant gave his replies exactly as if he had been an eyewitness to the grim events of that earlier day. The tension in the room heightened with the dawning realization that a real case might gell from this singular exercise in interrogation.

The clairvoyant paced back and forth across the room, the loop of wire spinning in his hands.

"It was so," he said. "Four went into the house. One stayed outside in the car. He is the short one, who went to his home. He is no killer. He is very frightened. . . ."

Then to the amazement of the officers, the clairvoyant moved back a few paces. "Watch," he said. "This is the one. I'll imitate him. He walks like this, see, with a limp. His left leg is a little shorter than his right leg. He is shorter than I am, and I am five feet six. He went to the house we went to, in the pick-up truck."

While he spoke, the clairvoyant strode back and forth in a limping gait. It was not the way he usually walked.

Then, abruptly, his manner of walking changed again, drastically. He moved out with his shoulders pulled back and his arms swinging in a rangy, loose-limbed, athletic gait few short men can manage. Some gear seemed to have shifted in his body, in his muscular and nervous systems. My imagination might have been deceiving me, but he seemed to be actually taller! He was the same person, yet somehow we were watching a totally different person.

"I'm imitating the tall one now," he said. "The killer. He is all right in his general health but he suffers from hemorrhoids and they bother him all the time. Also he spits a lot, every few seconds. He is the one who works at the tire place. He was in Vietnam and killed there, many times, with the garrote."

The officers exchanged glances. The sheriff nodded to the chief of police and I was certain they had given a name to this tall killer.

"You must understand I don't accuse anyone," the clairvoyant stated. "I am just a psychic and can tell only what I see. You have to put it together your own way."

Then he went on to describe—and to imitate in his fantastic way—each member of the killing party. Countless details of their lives flowed from the seemingly bottomless well of information about this months-old crime that was somehow contained within his mind. He *knew*. He talked about careers, marriages and families, states of physical and mental health, military service. He revealed motives, plans, plots, meetings, arguments, conspiracies, and weaknesses. He described the relationships between the killers and between the killers and victims.

It went on and on. He described houses, vehicles, getaway routes, even the rooms in which he envisioned principles of the case living. He stated categorically that two of the killers were seen and spoken to by outsiders who will remember them.

Still determined to remain detached, I asked myself if it was an act—an elaborate charade, complete with script and choreography, arising out of an uncommonly inventive mind backed up by an extraordinary memory?

But if it was an act, for whose benefit was it being played? Not mine, surely, and not Jim Bolton's. The officers, then? But if this was so, he was running the risk of almost instant repudiation. Some of the details were so explicit they could be verified in hours or less.

Yet if it was not an act, then the clairvoyant's actions and statements were being dictated by some mysterious and unknowable inner force—surely, some power that existed in his mind alone.

There was a momentary lull. Some confusion over terms was cleared up. Then the clairvoyant made a statement that lifted the sheriff right out of his chair!

Shots were fired in the house, the clairvoyant said. None of the victims had been shot, but he insisted that shots were fired.

If a mountain of a man can be said to gape, the sheriff gaped. "How many shots?" he demanded.

"Two," the clairvoyant replied. "It was so. You found two bullets. One in the wall and the other in the floor. Two shots were fired to scare the people."

The sheriff slumped down into his chair again like a wounded mammoth. He glanced at each of his fellow officers, then returned his gaze to the psychic. "Well, I don't know how you do it," he said. "But you sure are right on that one. We did find two bullets in the house."

Then, reluctantly, as though the feeling still lingered that such impossible things should be left in the realm of the impossible, the officers began to admit the accuracy of other details pointed out by the clairvoyant.

Some of them were minor but nonetheless significant: the arrangement of furniture in the now-empty house; the positions of the bodies; the time of the killings; the instrument of strangulation. . . .

Then one detail more startling than the others was confirmed. The clairvoyant had said that one of the victims died not from strangulation but from heart failure brought on by sheer terror— and the sheriff revealed that the autopsy report agreed! Yet the clairvoyant had never seen the bodies, and the newspapers had reported that all the victims had been strangled!

The effect of all this on the officers may be imagined. Hard-headed and phlegmatic men as they were, married to their job with its tough, investigative methods and welded into their rugged mountain environment, they scratched their heads in bemusement at the scenes they witnessed and the statements they heard. But as the confirmable facts were confirmed, they took a hard look at their case and the new countenance it had suddenly assumed.

They had reached an impasse. They had had no real lead or theory, but now, out of the blue and out of the mind of a man who had been hundreds of miles away the night the murders were committed, they suddenly found themselves not only with dozens of leads and clues but—if they could prove it—the whole story.

No one could be convicted, of course, on the say-so of the clairvoyant, but he had opened crevices in the brick wall the police had encountered, and there was a good chance he had knocked it down completely. On the face of it he had offered them no more than a theory, but it was a theory studded with verifiable details and some of them had already been verified. If it was not a theory based on facts and reality, then coincidence had been stretched far beyond its normal limits. And if the police, using their own investigative methods, could prove the theory correct, then it was certain that a band of desperate killers was at large only temporarily.

The police could interview the night waitress at the hamburger stand. They could verify that cars had been parked in particular places at particular times. Above all, they could concentrate on the suspects described by the clairvoyant and identified by the officers themselves. I felt I would not have liked to have been in the shoes of any of those people.

Then, as we were preparing to leave, an incident took place that seemed to add a point of punctuation to the whole remarkable exercise. The officers, talking among themselves, mentioned a name. It was the name of a man—a local lawyer—we had not seen or met that day.

The clairvoyant turned, set himself, and strode across the room in yet another totally different manner of walking—ducking his head and coughing into his cupped hand.

"Is this the fellow?" he asked, smiling. "A fat fellow? Cigar smoker? Coughs a lot, like this?"

The officers, startled this time into laughter, shook their heads one last time in bewilderment.

"Yes, sir. That's the one, all right."

The name of the clairvoyant is Marinus Bernardus Dykshoorn. This is his story.

RUSSELL FELTON

Toronto, Canada, 1974

I

THE GIFT AND THE BEGINNINGS

I was born clairvoyant and my earliest memories are, I suspect, psychic memories. By this I mean that many of the things I recall most vividly from my early childhood did not happen to me at all, but happened to other people. I became aware of them, and so remember them, through my psychic abilities, which were as strong in me then as they are now.

For example, when I was no older than five, I witnessed a suicide, and while my memories of my actual life at that time are quite fuzzy and indistinct, I can recall that event even now with vivid clarity.

I was standing at the window of my parents' home in the small Dutch town of Honselersdijk, looking out over the scene of our street. It was winter and the snow was falling heavily. I could barely make out the houses facing ours. There was nothing to watch but the snow falling.

Yet as I watched, I saw a man enter a barn. Inside the barn I saw him take a length of rope and hang himself from a beam.

But it did not happen, and I had not seen it at all. I had seen

· the snow falling on the street, and nothing else. You could not see fifty yards through that snow. Furthermore, our house was in town. There were no barns to be seen from our window, even on a clear day.

I couldn't understand it. I knew the incident had occurred because I had seen it and a child believes what he sees. I had seen a man hang himself. But now the snow was falling again and there were no people on the street and I was frightened.

I ran and told my father what I had seen, but his reaction was to become angry. I was imagining things, he said, and my imagination must have struck him as being diabolic. A daydreaming five-year-old ought to have been conjuring up more pleasant images. I was punished—because to be truthful this was not the first outlandish story I had recounted to my parents out of my "imagination"—and the punishment only added to my confusion.

But the worst shock came later—for both my father and myself. No one had hanged himself that day in our district, and no one had done so in the recent past. It was two weeks *later* that it happened. At a farm several miles from our home, a man hanged himself in his barn. From a beam. Exactly as I had described it to my father. And it was the same man I had seen in my "daydream."

Who can explain it? It still astonishes even me. I am psychic. I possess certain abilities of the mind—psychic abilities—that I call my gift and that enable me to see, hear, and know things I should not be able to see, hear, or know if I possessed only the five "normal" senses of sight, hearing, touch, taste, and smell.

My difference from other people is that I possess each of the five "normal" senses to a psychic degree. I am clairvoyant, but I am also clairaudient and my gift enables me to see, hear, feel, taste, and even smell things removed from me in both space and time.

I was born with these abilities, and through my life they have remained at a constant level of potency. Yet, although they are an intrinsic part of me, I really know very little about them. I cannot tell you why I possess them and other people do not, or through what accident of birth I acquired them, or even how they work within my own mind.

My gift has dominated my life and, although it exists within my own mind, it exists as a separate part, a part which I, Rien Dykshoorn, have never been able to penetrate. Perhaps because it has always been a part of me, I have never been able to rationalize it or explain it in terms anyone else can understand. Certainly I have never learned *why* I have it, or what it is in itself, or for what purpose it was given to me.

The most I have ever been able to do is come to terms with it in my own conscious mind and learn to turn it to purposes to which it lends itself, to work with it in the real world. Yet though I have been able to tap its energies in this way, even though I have applied my gift to thousands of problems and questions, and even though it has sustained me unfailingly for a quarter of a century, I still know as little about it as I did when I was a child.

It still amazes me. Even now, whenever I tell someone something I have learned through my gift, and it turns out that what I have said is true, I am astonished. I think to myself: *How? Why?*

All my life I have been searching for the answers to these two questions.

My concern is for parapsychology, which is the study of the paranormal, of psychic phenomena and what might be called the visible, audible, or tangible manifestations of unknown forces. My gift is an unknown force; its nature, origins, and purposes are completely mysterious, even to me.

My gift is, however, quite real. It generates psychic phenomena that can be seen, heard, and verified. It causes things to happen that would not happen if only known, identifiable forces were at work. So I am a practical parapsychologist; I am one of the people other parapsychologists study, and I am also a serious student of my own field.

In my native Netherlands, in Australia, where I lived for nine years, and in the United States I have been tested and examined by parapsychologists, and by psychologists, psychiatrists, biologists, geneticists, neurologists, cardiologists, and all kinds of doctors and scientists as well as various self-styled experts in the field of ESP. But none has ever been able to explain to me what my gift is, or how it works.

We know only that it does work and can be seen to work. No one can explain *how* it works, but it does, and to a certain extent both the parapsychologists and I have had to be content with that.

In the Netherlands and in Belgium I was tested many times at universities—among them the universities of Amsterdam, Delft, and Utrecht—and was found to be a bona fide, or genuine, psychic. The researchers concluded that, although my abilities could not be explained, they could be seen to work and I was allowed to practice as a professional clairvoyant.

At the same time, the results I achieved in my work were public knowledge and I was accepted by the press, the police, the public, and finally the government as a genuine clairvoyant capable of performing a valuable service to the community. Always, it was the reality of my gift that was credited, with the theorizing about its nature and origins taking second place to its obvious practical value.

As far as I am concerned, this situation remains unchanged. I am a professional clairvoyant, and while it is important that we should try to learn how I do what I do, the most important thing is the work itself.

For the record, I was born July 10, 1920, in the Dutch provincial town of s'Gravenzande, and was christened Marinus Bernardus after my paternal and maternal grandfather. My father's name was Jacobus, my mother's, Lena. She had been Lena van der Houwen before she married my father in 1919.

s'Gravenzande is in the below–sea-level area of the Netherlands known as Westland, just inland from the dyke-fortified coastline between The Hague and the Hook of Holland. The region is criss-crossed with canals and waterways and the principal industry consists of supplying hothouse-cultivated fruit and vegetables to all of Holland and parts of Belgium and Germany. The chief means of transporting produce from the hothouses was by canal barges and boats and it was on one of these boats, owned by my grandfather, that my father worked at the time I was born.

In the summer of 1921 we moved to Honselersdijk, only a matter of three or four miles away, and it was here that I grew up.

I would like to be able to say that my childhood and youth were happy times, but they were not. From the earliest years of my life, virtually from the time I first became aware of my environment and learned to speak, I was constantly in trouble, confused and bewildered by the goings-on in my mind. This state of personal affairs was to last until I was almost thirty, and it came close to ruining my life.

I have already pointed out that my gift made itself evident very early in my life, and that it led me into trouble by bringing me psychic impressions neither I nor my parents could cope with or understand. I witnessed the suicide, yet I did not in a sense, for none had taken place, and certainly none that I could have seen from our home. Yet I *had* seen it, and being a child I told my father about it. But the telling made him angry and he punished me by sending me to my room. Then later my impression was proved to be valid and true. I *had* seen it, but I had seen it *before* it happened.

This cycle of events was repeated many times, and not only when dramatic or tragic incidents took place in our community. My gift was just as accurate in trivial matters: I remember once when I was about six, making my way home through our town and encountering a lady cleaning the windows of her store. I stopped to watch her for a while, and as I watched I suddenly knew that she and her husband had been out on the town the night before. I saw them laughing and drinking and dancing, and because I saw nothing wrong in it, I told her about it.

The next thing I knew she had jumped down from her ladder,

firmly gripped my ear and started hauling me along the street toward my home. There she told my mother in no uncertain terms what she thought of our family. If my mother and father felt they had to discuss her affairs, she said, they should at least not do so in front of their son. She took offense, she said, at having her private activities broadcast in the street.

So I was punished again, and not only for speaking out of turn. My parents assumed, naturally enough, that I had been sneaking out at night and, worse, had been hanging around the taverns. How else could I have known about the woman's night of carousing?

This happened time and time again as my gift let me in on other people's secrets. Once I told a friend of my mother's that I "saw a little baby in her tummy." I didn't realize this was not the kind of thing one said to a lady; I was trying to be polite.

My special talent manifested itself in other ways. For one thing, my parents could never surprise me with a gift for Christmas or my birthday. Merely by realizing I was going to receive a gift, I knew what the gift was going to be. I never went "gift-hunting" as impatient children will, because it wasn't necessary. Knowing that Christmas was approaching, and knowing that my parents would buy me a gift, I would also know the exact moment that gift was brought into the house, and I would simply go and claim it. The word "surprise" had no meaning for me because I was aware even before my parents what my gift would be, and once it was in the house I knew exactly where it was hidden. I would "see" it in its hiding place.

In the same way, I could always find things around the house. If the word "surprise" had no meaning for me, neither did the word "lost." Whenever anything was missing in the house, I would go and find it. Not by searching, nor by remembering where the object had been left, but merely by thinking about it. I always imagined that whenever my parents said something was "lost," they meant for me to find and bring it to them. This would bring into my mind a clear image of the missing object in its physical location—whether it was in the bottom of a closet, under a chair, or discarded with the garbage.

But my ability to find things, like my insights into the lives of friends and neighbors, always brought me trouble. If I found something in the house, it was always automatically assumed that I had also hidden it, and that I was responsible for its having been lost in the first place. Or if I found a gift, it was assumed that I had carried out a systematic search, and so I was punished again.

My parents could not be blamed, of course. They had no idea they had produced a psychic child. Even if the possibility had been suggested to them, they would not have been able to understand the concept, much less interpret my childish behavior as positive indications of clairvoyance. The word would have had virtually no meaning for them. Ours was a simple, rural community of people who worked hard and thought straight and kept their lives uncomplicated and expected everyone else to do the same.

I can understand now what a source of worry and frustration I must have been to my parents. Many years later they would see me work in public and would understand how it had always been with me. But when I was young they could not have been expected to understand why I was a "problem child." It is the duty of parents to punish a child when he misbehaves, and from my parents' point of view, I certainly misbehaved very often.

The punishments did not improve my behavior simply because I did not know what offenses I had committed. You must remember that I was born clairvoyant, and had no yardstick of normality by which to judge my behavior or my thoughts. I did not realize there were things I should not have known. I did not realize I was in any way different from anyone else.

But I was different, and inevitably I became more withdrawn, more isolated from the people around me. The only way I could stay out of trouble was by keeping quiet, and so I kept quiet. The long and difficult process of estrangement from the world had begun even before I had come into real contact with it.

That contact came when I started school, and if my gift had

made my life difficult up till then, from that point on it made my life a misery.

By relating various incidents and circumstances in which my gift brought me specific information, I may have given the impression that it made itself evident only sporadically, whenever I concentrated on a particular person or object, or that it worked in reaction to events in my own life. But this was not the case. In fact, the crucial problem of my youth was that the psychic part of my mind was operating almost constantly, and I could not control it.

This is very difficult to explain. But if the human mind can be said to consist of a conscious and a subconscious, and if the conscious dominates the subconscious in determining how we behave from day to day, then it might be said that when I was young my mental situation was the reverse of the normal. My psychic gift, contained somewhere within my subconscious, dominated my conscious mind, constantly bombarding my conscious thoughts with psychic impressions. And because I had no yardstick of normality by which to judge my thoughts, I could not distinguish between these psychic impressions and the reality of my every day world.

I was born psychic, but no one knew it, least of all myself. At first, I was not even aware that I was different from other people, but I soon found out that I was. Other people considered me "strange." I was a rude, impudent, spying, eavesdropping child, given to making wildly imaginative statements about all manner of things. It does not take long, when everyone calls you strange, to realize that you *are* different.

But even as I began to realize that my thought processes were different from those of the people around me, I still could not comprehend the nature of the difference. How much was I supposed to know, and how much was I not? I had no way of telling, and no one else could tell me, because they did not understand how *my* mind worked.

I could not control my subconscious. Images, impressions, sights, sounds, smells, and even tastes came flooding into my mind spontaneously, unheralded, and uninvited. I did not need to concentrate on another person to know about him—I knew *instinctively*. The psychic impressions flooded up from my subconscious, and there was no way I could stop them or even control the flow.

Then there was the problem of *what* I learned about other people. I was a child, but through the automatic workings of my gift I learned things a child could not possibly understand, and these things confused and frightened me. Yet every time I sought help or explanation, I only invited punishment because—naturally enough—it was assumed that I had obtained my information by devious means.

It was a complex, difficult situation. I always knew, for example, when someone was lying to me, and I could not understand why anyone would say something that was patently not true. Surely everyone else realized there was no truth in what was being said?

Everything added to my reputation as being a "strange one." I was tactless because I did not realize there are lies no one wants revealed. I was rude, insulting friends, relatives, neighbors, and the most innocent callers.

As I said, all these things caused me to withdraw into myself though it was not in my nature to withdraw. I wanted to make friends and I wanted to help people. Very often I could see illness or injury or unhappiness approaching for individuals I liked, and because I cared about them, I would try to warn them. Of course, they could not understand my warnings because they could not believe that I knew, so I was powerless even to use the knowledge I had. And so I withdrew.

But at school I could not withdraw, and my emotional troubles began in earnest. For the first time in my life I found myself obliged to sit for hours on end in the same room with twenty or more other people.

Picture the scene: The teacher is reading a story and the class is attentive, waiting to hear the outcome. One boy, however, sits staring fixedly at the teacher's face. He already knows the outcome of the story and cannot realize the others do not. Why is the teacher reading the story when everyone knows what will happen and there is no truth in it anyway? None of it ever happened.

The boy sits in silence because he has to—but his mind is buzzing. Today as every day it whirls in confusion, filled with incomprehensible and often frightening images, sounds, smells, tastes, impressions, and sensations. He sees his classmates not only as they are now, but as they have been and as they will be in the future. And he sees their parents, friends, relatives—people he has never met—and he knows them, too.

He knows that one of his friends will fall and break his arm. The mother of another friend is very ill but does not know it. What can he say? He has already learned from experience that there are things one cannot say, but he cannot distinguish between what he should know and what he should not. Without wanting to or trying to, he knows every person in the classroom.

He stares at the teacher's face. He knows her. He knows her parents, friends, her future husband, their children. Perhaps she is ill, or will be—he feels nauseous. . . .

If he cannot stand the whirling in his mind, if he breaks under the strain, if he jumps up and runs out, he only adds to his already formidable reputation as a "strange one."

This instinctive, unwilling involvement with the lives of people around me, which became unbearable whenever I was obliged to mix with groups over long periods of time, was to become the dominant problem of my life and eventually induced me to lead the life I have. I would overcome it, but not without a great deal of difficulty, and not without some help from unexpected quarters.

In the meantime I grew up, and with the help of some sympathetic teachers I did manage to pass through school. By this time, however, other problems, totally unrelated to my own, had risen to engulf our family, our country, and the world.

My father had been able to buy a boat and branch out on his own, but before he had time to consolidate this new start, the depression hit. Then an extremely severe winter froze the canals and from that point on the story was all too common for those times: no boat, no job, and very little money.

It was against this background that I finished school and started looking for work. I was fourteen years old.

2

WORK, WAR, AND WORRY

I found work as an odd-job boy in a complex of Honselersdijk hothouses. One of my duties was to clean out the flues of the intricate steam-heating system. I was the only employee small enough to crawl into the flues with a bucket and brush. In the off season I spent most of my days crawling into ducts and boilers, while in the high season I swept, cleaned, and, among other things, blew the time whistle.

The owner was a Mr. Vreugdenhill and he, unexpectedly, became one of the first people to help me out of my psychological and emotional difficulties.

He encouraged me to read, and for this simple act I will remain grateful to him as long as I live, because books became the medium through which I was able to understand much of what I had seen of human behavior. I had come to realize that my mind was different, and I was no longer surprised by the psychic impressions that slipped of their own accord into my conscious thoughts, but the things I saw in other people's lives continued to trouble and confuse me. Why did people act the way they did? Why did they insist on complicating their lives? And why did they resent it so much when I revealed to them what I knew about them?

I don't know why, but the basic reading list Mr. Vreugdenhill drew up for me included some of the works of Freud and Jung, the pioneers of modern psychology and psychiatry. Perhaps he discerned something in me that no one else ever had—a consuming interest in human motivation and behavior that perhaps he took as an academic interest that could be furthered by reading. At any rate, these works, although they were heavy going for a teen-ager without even a higher school education, helped me a great deal.

The second thing Mr. Vreugdenhill did was to encourage me to further my formal education. He may have had the future of his own business in mind, but in any case he was instrumental in having me enroll in an evening course in agriculture at the college in s'Gravenzande.

I completed this course in two years, then followed it with an-other two years studying accounting and bookkeeping.

During this time I remained introspective and reserved, still puzzled by the workings of my mind. My tenuous familiarity with some of the principles of psychology helped me to rationalize some of the things I learned from my gift, but not to explain how or why I was able to know them. And my gift continued to intrude on my personal relationships. I made friends and lost them, alienating them with my extrasensory knowledge, which I could never keep concealed for very long because I could never resist the urge to help, warn, or encourage people with whom I was acquainted. If I saw a friend hesitating over a decision, and I knew what the outcome would be, I could not help trying to advise him. Or if I foresaw trouble, I could not help issuing a warning.

But friendships, I discovered, hung on slender threads. Advice should be given only if sought. My friends always demanded to know *how* I knew about their problems, and I could never ex-plain. Friendships would end in arguments and recriminations—

I was a nosy Parker, an eavesdropper, a spy. So finally I kept myself aloof, avoiding close personal relationships.

Then, one evening in early 1938, came the first real turning point of my life. I read in a newspaper from The Hague that a certain Professor Greven, a professor of psychology and parapsychology from the University of Cologne, was scheduled to deliver a public lecture entitled: "Dreams, Clairvoyance and Supernatural Phenomena."

I went along. I don't know why, but I was drawn by destiny to that lecture. Certainly I had no particular interest in the subject of the lecture. The word "clairvoyance" touched no particular chord in me at the time. My mental impressions did not come to me in dreams, but in broad daylight. Yet I went to the lecture, riding my bicycle to The Hague.

Professor Greven was totally blind, and had devoted a lifetime of study to the intricacies of the human mind. He could not see his audience, yet he knew more about them than they knew themselves. And extraordinarily enough, he knew me! He knew my problem, and when he spoke of psychic abilities, he was talking about mine!

I was stunned. This blind old man, then in his seventies, knew more about me than I knew myself. For the first time I began to realize—and to hope—that my situation might not be totally beyond explanation.

After the lecture I sought him out. I sensed that he was the only man in the world who could help me get rid of the feeling that had troubled me all my life—the feeling that I could not control my own mind.

I waited until the hall was almost empty, then approached him and tried to explain my problem. He listened without a word. After what seemed a terribly long time, he began asking me questions. How did I "see" the things I "saw"? Did my feelings distress me physically? Did they intensify when I was tired? Were they heightened by my sense of touch?

I told him everything, and when I was finished he gave me a startling explanation. He told me that I seemed to be highly "psychic"—that I possessed a paranormal faculty, a capacity for clairvoyance, a "gift."

"From what you tell me," he said, "your gift is inborn, and very highly developed. It presents you with very unusual problems. You will have to learn to live with it."

But I did not want to learn to live with it—I wanted to get rid of it. I did not want to be "clairvoyant," I wanted to be normal. My "gift," if that's what it was, had been the cause of every unhappy experience of my life. I wanted only to be free of it.

"It is highly unlikely that you will ever be rid of it," Professor Greven told me. "You may be able to suppress it, but probably not for very long. My advice to you is to learn to live with it and to control it, and then I would advise you to use it."

Use it? It took me a while to comprehend what he was suggesting—that I should become a clairvoyant, a practitioner of ESP.

"But all I want is to get rid of it!" I said.

Professor Greven smiled. "Rien," he said, "if we knew how to get rid of such a gift, then we would also know how to get it—and we don't."

After that I met with Professor Greven many times. He became a friend and helped me more than any man before or since—but still I ignored his advice. He wanted me to become a professional clairvoyant. He said there would be no other way, finally, for me. He told me that I might be able to perform very valuable work, for my friends about whom I was constantly worried, and for the community. He told me I was lucky to have been born in the Netherlands, where the attitude toward ESP was considerably more enlightened than in most countries.

"You will still meet skepticism and hostility," he said. "Many people will call you a fraud, a charlatan, even a freak. You must expect that. But what do they call you now? Spy and eavesdropper. And at least you will be able to turn your abilities to valuable purposes. Think of the friends you want to help, but cannot. Do you not owe it to them to help them, and others like them?"

But I ignored his advice. He was a kindly, sympathetic man but he lived, I felt, in his own world where psychics were accepted. I was the son of hard-working parents, born into a small, rural community. I was expected to settle into a respectable job and live a normal life, and this was what I wanted to do. I was not about to put aside my hard-won qualifications to set myself up as a professional exponent of clairvoyance. Not even if I could succeed at it, which I doubted.

So I went back to the hothouses, and in 1939 I enrolled in yet another evening course—in economics and statistics—at the college in The Hague.

Through all this period, while I was concerned with my personal difficulties, Europe was having problems that would soon involve all of us, and by April of 1940 those problems had swelled and erupted. Hitler's armies had already occupied Poland and Czechoslovakia and were engaged in a full-scale invasion of Norway and Denmark. It was obvious he would soon turn his attentions westward, and the world waited to see exactly when and where he would strike.

The mood in Holland was hopeful. Editorial opinion was optimistic. Many felt that because of our neutrality in 1914–18 and our waterline defense system, the Germans would leave us alone. Also, of course, Hitler had only months before repeated his assurances that the neutrality of both Holland and Belgium would be respected.

At dawn on May 10 the Germans unleashed a massive invasion of the largely unprepared Low Countries. Fully aware of the danger of a frontal assault bogging down in the floodable lowlands, Hitler unleashed the first full-scale airborne invasion in the history of warfare. Within five days his paratroopers, equipped with lightweight weapons and machinery, had occupied all the strategic points in Holland. Our forces offered stubborn but hopeless resistance, and on May 15 we capitulated.

These events, although they profoundly affected the lives of all the Dutch people, did not at first seriously disrupt my own rather mundane existence. I stayed at the hothouses and in 1941 enrolled in yet another evening course in The Hague, hoping to matriculate and perhaps go on to the university.

Then in 1942 I was seconded to the Ministry of Agriculture, assigned as an officer in charge of supervising the implementation of new regulations devised by the German occupiers.

They intended using Holland as a large vegetable garden, but they were obliged to leave much of the administration of their policies to the incumbent Dutch authorities. This meant that although the overall German instructions had to be carried out, the Dutch middle- and lower-level administrators were frequently able to assist them in dodging the rigid German rules. I joined the underground movement and worked in it until the end of the war. My part was to falsify reports of harvests and yields, diverting unreported produce to the active underground groups, who used it to feed partisans and the striking railroad workers. The Germans could not watch everything that came out of the ground, and if some of it was diverted before it was recorded they were never the wiser.

It was during this time, too, that I began relying on the impressions I received from my gift to keep myself and others out of trouble. I never told anyone about these impressions, but for the first time in my life I began paying attention to them and planning accordingly. In those days it paid to be cautious.

In 1943 I was transferred to The Hague and saw the war out from there. One evening the college was bombed flat, bringing an abrupt end to my studies there.

After the war life returned to normal. The free government returned and everyday business resumed.

I was promoted within the ministry to a desk job, then in 1946 to a career position in the section for statistics and planning. Everything seemed in order at last. I had settled into a secure job with reasonable pay, good prospects, and some status in the eyes of my friends.

But my contentment was short-lived. I was deskbound. A constant restlessness nagged me. My gift began to intrude more seriously than ever into my personal relationships, with painful and destructive consequences.

The old problem took root again. I knew too much about the people with whom I worked—and I still could not stem the flow of these psychic impressions.

Above all, I felt responsible for these people. I knew their problems, their worries, the cares that weighed them down. How could I not tell them and try to help them? How could I not try to prevent them from making disastrous mistakes or worrying themselves sick over problems I knew would soon be resolved? It was a repetition of the situation I had faced at school, but made worse by the fact that I *knew* I could help, if only there was any possibility that my friends would have believed the things I told them. Yet how many of them would have believed that I had obtained my knowledge of their personal lives "psychically"? And how many would have accepted any advice I might have offered? Not many, I realized.

The strain rapidly became intolerable. I could not confess my clairvoyance, nor could I restrain it in my own mind. Meanwhile, I had to live and work with these people day after day, week after week, month after month, knowing, sensing, feeling, and becoming involved with their personal problems. I realized I would have to resign from the ministry, for the sake of my own peace of mind.

So I did resign, abandoning my prospects of a solid career, and took a job as a sales representative with a vegetable-oil company in Delft, selling stock feed and nutrient by-products to farmers in the Amersfoort district.

I sold some, and certainly felt more at ease working alone and outside than at my ministry desk, but again it was not long before my gift played havoc with my working life.

The crunch came with an incident that seems amusing now, although it did not seem so at the time. As a free service to its customers, the company provided veterinarians, nutritionists, livestock experts, and the like as consultants. These men would visit the farmers from time to time to advise on problems or just help out in the interest of public relations. Salesmen accompanied them on their visits, to benefit from the farmers' good graces and pick up some specialized knowledge at the same time.

One day I accompanied one of these experts to a poultry farm. He was supposed to instruct me on some of the finer points of poultry farming, but I was to learn more about myself than about chickens.

Our task was to sort fertile chickens from the infertile and coop them separately. Each bird had to be carefully inspected to determine whether or not it was capable of laying eggs. The infertile were to be cooped for butchering.

The expert spent quite a long time explaining to me how to determine the fertility of a chicken, then he left me to carry on alone.

The instant I touched the first chicken, however, a very strange thing happened. As soon as I asked myself, mentally, "Is this chicken fertile?" I experienced something I can describe only as a "reaction" in my hands. It felt like a mild but very definite electric shock, and it was accompanied by a feeling of absolute certainty that this was, indeed, a fertile chicken. I had no need to examine the bird further; the "reaction" and the feeling of certainty were enough.

And so—probably foolishly—I set about using this "instinctive" method to sort the flock. Each time I picked up a bird, I asked myself, "Is this one fertile?" If I got the reaction, I knew it was. If there was no reaction, I cooped the bird as infertile.

In the first half hour I sorted more than one hundred birds.

Of course, when the expert returned to check my progress he said, "You couldn't have done so many so quickly! You haven't been inspecting them properly!"

"I don't know," I said. "But check them if you like."

He did—and the more birds he inspected, the angrier he grew. It took him hours, but he could find no bird in the wrong coop. The state of his humor may be imagined.

A week later I was summoned to the company's head office in Delft. The expert had submitted a scathing report on my loyalty, good manners, and willingness to learn the poultry trade. I was asked to resign and I complied.

I took a job as a bank clerk in Rotterdam. As it turned out, it was to be my last "normal" job.

3

THE PROFESSIONAL CLAIRVOYANT

I lasted four long, unhappy months at the bank. I had to work to support myself—having long since moved out of my parents' home to live alone—but I deeply regretted having lost my outside job. Once again, the old problem rose to plague me. I was back inside with the same people day after day, week after week. The strain became unbearable. It could not last.

This time help came from a totally unexpected quarter.

Working at my desk one afternoon, I suddenly received an extremely vivid psychic impression: I saw my supervisor in the bank manager's office, and the two of them were discussing me! I had made an error in calculation, and my supervisor was reporting it to the manager. I *knew* it; I saw and heard it.

I was overcome with indignation. The supervisor had not told me about my own mistake, and now he was asking the manager to fire me without even giving me the chance to defend myself. On an angry impulse I decided to do something about it.

The manager's office was equipped with a set of warning lights like traffic signals. When a red light shone over his door, he was not to be disturbed. The red light was on as I pushed open the door and strode straight into the office.

Needless to say, both men were astounded by this unprecedented intrusion. They were even more astonished when I told them what I thought of their conversation. But they were rendered speechless when—in reply to the obvious question—I told them that I had "overheard" them because I happened to be psychic!

This was, incidentally, the first time I had ever admitted to anyone that I was clairvoyant. Professor Greven had told me almost a decade earlier, but I had never once dared to reveal it to anyone else. Now, in my righteous anger, I blurted it out without ever intending to say it, but nevertheless I said it, and this may have been the true turning point of my life.

Five minutes later I was alone with the manager in his office. I expected to be fired. It had happened again. All that remained was for the formal announcement to be made.

But surprisingly enough, the manager did not fire me—at least, not summarily. He asked me about myself and my gift, and to my surprise he seemed genuinely interested. What had I meant by my claim that I was "psychic"? How had I known about his conversation with my supervisor?

I told him. I told him about Professor Greven and what he had said and I explained how and why I had lost my last job and could not stay in this one. I had been trying for years to suppress this psychic part of my mind, but it would not be suppressed.

Finally he suggested that I consult a psychologist.

"But I'm not crazy!" I protested.

"I wouldn't suggest that you are," he said. "Nor am I suggesting that you need psychiatric treatment. But you might be able to have this 'clairvoyance,' if that's what it is, further explained to you. As you have just said yourself, suppressing it doesn't seem to have helped very much."

Then he fired me—or at least we agreed that I could not stay with the bank. I left with two months' salary in lieu of notice and the name and address of a prominent Rotterdam psychologist. This was 1948 and I had been aware for almost ten years that I was clairvoyant. Now I was out on the street, unemployed, with nothing to look forward to but having my mental processes critically examined by a psychologist—a far from pleasant prospect.

Yet I also left the bank with a feeling of tremendous relief. It was out in the open now, and the matter would have to be resolved, once and for all time.

The interview with the psychologist began with a reaction test. Forewarned by the bank manager—who had made the appointment for me—that I claimed a psychic ability, the psychologist handed me a file containing a set of numbered photographs, asking me to state my immediate reaction to each picture in turn.

I took the file, but did not open it. Now, I thought, it's all in the hands of fate, or whatever this thing is that I have. Can I *use* it, to find out things I want to know, or decide that I want to know? Let's find out.

I took the file in my hands and *asked myself* what it contained. Photographs, of course. But of what? Objects? Symbols? People? People. What kind of people? Men? Women? Both? Both. What did they have in common?

Then I knew. I cannot explain how I knew—but I *knew*!

I said: "These are photographs of very disturbed people. Many of them are dead. I think all the pictures were taken in a hospital or an asylum."

The psychologist said nothing. He asked me to look at the first photograph. It showed a young woman standing on a lawn. Her hair had been cropped short and her expression was grim but vacant.

And I knew her. I saw her, heard her speak. I felt physical pain and knew that somehow it had been her pain. She had been dead for several years.

"This girl is dead," I told the psychologist. "For a long time before she died she was obsessed with the idea that she was suffering from an incurable disease. But there was nothing physically wrong with her. Doctors put her in an institution. She seemed to improve and they sent her home. A few weeks later she lapsed into a deep depression. Finally she jumped from the third-floor window of her home and was killed."

I examined eight photographs in all. Various testing methods were used to determine whether I needed to touch the photographs in any special way, or at all. I did not. In fact, I did not even need to see the picture on which I was concentrating. Nor did it make any difference whether or not the psychologist could see the picture. I was not reading his mind; on some of the subjects I gave him more information than he himself knew.

Then we talked, about my gift, my problems, Professor Greven, the fact that I did not need to exert any effort to make my gift function, but instead could not *stop* it from functioning. And the psychologist told me exactly what Professor Greven had told me almost a decade earlier: I was clairvoyant.

"You appear," he said, "to possess a paranormal or psychic ability—and a remarkably accurate one. I am familiar with the work of Professor Greven, and I believe I am aware of your emotional difficulties. You will probably never be able to adjust to living with people unless you learn to control your psychic ability. The strain will become more and more intense."

"Should I try to become a professional clairvoyant?" I asked.

He replied: "Why not? After all, you *are* clairvoyant, and you can do valuable work. Why shouldn't you earn your living at it?"

Now I must try to explain something that may be difficult to understand: how I learned to work with the wire.

I have been a professional clairvoyant since 1948. I work for clients, I lecture and demonstrate my gift in public, and I work on important cases for the police or other authorities. Over the years tens of thousands of people have seen me working. Probably not one of them has fully understood the significance of the wire.

When I work, when I concentrate my gift on a problem, I hold in my hands a length of thin wire bent into a loop. It turns around in my hands, but I do not make it turn. It is a divining rod—but it is more than that and less than that.

When I left the psychologist's office in Rotterdam, I knew that I would become a professional clairvoyant. Perhaps I had known it since Professor Greven had told me it had to be, but now the decision had been made. I had not made it—perhaps I could never have made that decision on my own—but it had been made and I had no choice except to live with it. I felt tremendously relieved, as though an enormous weight had been lifted from my shoulders. The issue was resolved. My gift could be *used*. That was enough for me.

One major difficulty remained, however. Although I now knew the energies of my gift could be turned to directions of my own choosing, I still had no control over them. My gift had always been my master, functioning at random and almost constantly. Now I had to learn to become its master, to turn it on when I needed it and turn it off when I didn't need it—the second task being the more difficult. I had to learn to relax in my mind.

The wire was the instrument I chose. I can't explain *why*, any more than I can explain *how* it turns my gift on and off. The wire has no power of its own; it is not a talisman or a symbolic object, it is merely an aid to my concentration. I can work without it, but I prefer not to, because it took me a long time to get accustomed to working with it.

In Rotterdam I rented a room and stayed there for almost four months, trying to discipline myself to the point where I could concentrate my gift on specific questions at will, sustain the concentration, and then relax. I had to reach the stage at which when I wanted to concentrate, I could pick up the wire and the energy of my gift would flow, and when I wanted to get out of my psychic frame of mind, I could do it simply by setting the wire aside.

Not that I chose the wire arbitrarily. There were practical considerations. At twenty-eight I was setting out on a career in a field about which I was virtually ignorant. I did not know what I was going to do with my gift—but I knew some things I was *not* going to do. I would not become an "entertainer," a sideshow performer in top hat and tails, raising laughs with tricks and passing the hat. Nor would I set myself up as a mystic, exploiting the gullible with mumbo jumbo. Professor Greven had spelled it out: I had to become a *working* clairvoyant. I had to *use* my gift, turning it to purposes valuable to both individuals and society.

Through trial and experimentation, I found I could divine for water, and since water-diviners, or "dowsers," were respected for their obvious abilities in the surrounding rural districts, I thought I might support myself this way, at least for a while. Since most dowsers used a standard tool—a forked twig—I took a thin length of piano wire and bent it into the shape of a forked twig. It would be my divining rod, my aid to concentration.

However, by the time I had mastered the technique of dowsing, I had another problem. I was broke. I was faced, finally, with the *necessity* of earning money with my gift. I reached the point where I could not afford another week's rent.

I was procrastinating, of course. I was terrified of being ridiculed or scorned. I simply could not venture out into the countryside and offer my services to those hard-nosed farmers. What if one took me for a con man, or a roving thief?

So I hung around. Finally desperation was the mother of action. On the afternoon of September 24, 1948, I walked into a Rotterdam coffee house with exactly the price of one cup of coffee in my pocket.

The owner was serving behind the counter. He was a large, balding, unfriendly looking man, and I will never forget him—nor the baleful eye he turned on me as I spent my last coin on his coffee.

He turned to go. I took the divining rod out of my pocket. "Listen, sir," I said, "don't worry about your gall bladder operation. Everything will be all right and you'll be back here working again in less than six weeks. . . ."

He had started walking away. Now he stopped short, slowly turned and gave me a long, hard, cold look. "What was that?" he asked. "What did you say?"

This was the moment. I felt a huge desire to flee back to my room—anywhere! But I could not move, and I heard my voice say: "I am clairvoyant. It's my job. I saw you were worried by your illness, but it will be all right. Do you have any other problems I might help you with?"

For what seemed a long time he just stared at me. Then at last he said: "I should say I do. Listen, come to the back and let's hear what you have to say."

He led me through to his home in the back of the café, and here I performed my first consultation for a client. I was so nervous that I cannot remember a thing about it.

It must have gone well though, because afterward he introduced me to every customer who walked into the café that afternoon, and I worked for them all. That night I left with enough cash to pay my rent for two weeks.

After that I became the "resident clairvoyant" at the café, working for the customers. A few weeks later, the proprietor offered me the use of an upstairs room as a consulting office. Before long people started telephoning for appointments. Then my early clients started coming back for further consultations. Suddenly I was in business, and my gift had started to come into its own.

It was only now, too, as I found myself working every day with my gift, that I began to discover the range of uses that could be found for it. Increasingly I learned that I could "ask questions of myself" and learn the answers instinctively. It is difficult to explain, but faced with a possible set of alternative answers to a particular question, I would get a compelling feeling of certainty that one was right and the others were not.

I also found that I could look into the lives not only of people, but into the "lives" of buildings as well. Concentrating on an old house, for example, I would have strong psychic impressions of people who had lived there before—in the recent past, and even far back in history.

The discovery of this ability inside myself fascinated me, and I started spending my spare time seeking out old buildings to examine in this fashion. In particular, I went out of my way to visit places of historic interest—castles, ancient towns and seaports, medieval churches, the sites of the many historic events of my country—and, strange as it may seem, in my mind I was able to witness some of these historic events as they actually happened.

Then in October, 1948, this interest in history took me to Delft, the ancient Dutch town famous for its Delft-ware china, its quiet, picturesque waterways, and its Prinsenhof Museum. The Prinsenhof had once been a royal palace, and for my own amusement I was hoping to unlock some of its secrets.

When I arrived at the museum, I noticed a small team of workmen carefully reconstructing an old wall that had begun to crumble. The bricks of this old wall captured my attention, and I took out the divining rod to determine their age. They had been fired over four hundred years earlier.

As I was standing there holding the wire a man approached and asked what I was doing. From his neat suit and air of authority I guessed he had a right to ask, so I said: "I am a clairvoyant. I am finding out how old these bricks are."

The man smiled, but by now I had become accustomed to every possible reaction to my claims of clairvoyance. I did not mind skepticism because I was no longer ashamed of my gift.

Then the man said: "I see, you are psychic, are you? Well, I am the director of the museum. Perhaps you can tell me how old these bricks are."

"About four hundred years," I said.

He nodded. "Then perhaps you can also tell me where they came from."

That was easy. I led the way around the building until we

came to a narrow dividing wall made from the same type of brick. "You took the top layer of bricks from this wall to repair the other," I said.

Now the director became interested. "Listen," he said, "if you really are psychic, can you tell me where we might find more of these bricks—I mean of the same age and type—elsewhere in Delft?"

"Well, I will try," I said.

He took me inside the Prinsenhof to his office, where he showed me a detailed map of Delft. I was not certain how I was going to do the job, but I took the divining rod in my hands and moved it over the map, just as if I was diving for water over a field, waiting for some kind of reaction or psychic impression from my gift.

It came when the loop of the wire suddenly snapped upward from a point on the map, and I knew that at this place there were old bricks—of exactly the same type as were used in the Prinsenhof.

This happened four times, indicating that there were similar bricks at four different sites in the town.

"We will investigate all the sites," the director said. "If you are right, I will send you a fee."

Then he took me on a guided tour of the museum, but along the way he brought up another subject. "Are you familiar," he asked, "with the story of the assassination of Willem the Silent?"

I knew as much as any Dutch schoolboy. Willem the Silent, first prince of Orange and founder of the Royal Dutch dynasty, had lived in the Prinsenhof when it was a royal palace. He had been assassinated there in 1584 by one Balthaser Gérard. Gérard, who committed the assassination under instructions from Philip II of Spain, was arrested shortly afterward by palace guards, but angry crowds burst into the palace and wrought their own justice on the assassin. They dragged him into the open square and roped each of his limbs to a different horse. Gérard was torn apart.

This much was history. The director wanted to know whether

I could reveal any details of the assassination or the people involved. Of course, I was even more curious than he was, because I wanted to know whether I could do it.

We went into the chamber where the killing was known to have taken place, and I concentrated on the action. Immediately I knew what had happened. Willem had been shot once in the throat, and another shot had missed. Both bullets had lodged in the stone wall.

On the wall of the chamber was a small glass-fronted case protecting two neat holes from the potentially damaging fingers of sightseers. "These holes were originally much lower down," I said.

The director smiled. "If you are a trickster," he said, "you have certainly done your homework. How else has the room changed?"

"The floor was much lower," I said. "This is not the original floor. The level we are on would have been at about chest height in those days."

"Excellent!" he beamed. "You're absolutely right!"

But I was much more interested in testing my gift than impressing the director. I set out to reconstruct everything that had happened on that dark day for Holland in 1584.

"Gérard really did do it," I said. "Philip had promised him instant elevation to the Spanish nobility if he succeeded." (Willem, originally a Catholic, had supported Philip in his war against Henry II of France. Later, after William had converted to Protestanism, he opposed Philip in the Spanish king's persecution of Protestants.)

"Gérard gained an appointment with Willem," I said, "to request permission to leave the country for Spain. Without such a permit he could not have escaped to collect his reward. so he waited until Willem had signed the document before firing the shots." I walked over to the wall. "There was a doorway here, lower down. Gérard escaped through it and hid under a dung heap outside. When the guards found him, they brought him back inside and walled him up in another chamber. They hoped to preserve him from the mob, at least until he could be tried and made to confess to having acted for Philip. But some of the crowd noticed the new brickwork. They tore down the wall and took him."

For me this was a fascinating exercise, and the director must have been satisfied with the results, because he waived his condition of bricks first, fee later, and paid me on the spot the sum of one hundred guilders (about $30), for "clairvoyant services rendered."

But that was not the end of it. The next time I was in Delft I called on the director again. He told me that old bricks had been found on each of the sites I had pinpointed on the map of Delft. They appeared to have all been baked in the same kiln as the bricks of the Prinsenhof wall—approximately four hundred years earlier.

4

THE SEARCH FOR THE HOST
OF NIERVAART

Until now, in relating the problems of my youth and how I was able, finally, to resolve them, I have asked the reader to believe, without seeing proof, certain things about myself: that I was born clairvoyant; that my gift was strong in me throughout; that I saw, heard, felt, and knew things by psychic means; that ultimately I had no choice but to become a professional clairvoyant.

I have had very particular and important reasons for dwelling so long on this part of my life. I am not a parapsychologist, but my concern is for parapsychology, the study of extrasensory perception and its implications.

I am aware that many psychics claim a religious or mystic base for their gifts in the sense that they believe they have been directly gifted by God with their abilities and that, because they are "closer to God" than other people, they should be regarded as religious leaders. I reject this line of thinking altogether.

Personally, I am a religious man. I believe in God, and so I believe that my psychic gift originated with God—but only in the sense that all things originate with Him. When I say I am

47

"gifted," I mean no more than that I am gifted as writers, artists, singers, and musicians are said to be "gifted." I do not wish to be considered a religious leader; I am just a fellow human being and no closer to God than anyone else. My gift did not come to me as a "blessing" from God. He does not hold personal conversations with me, nor do I see visions of Him or of Christ. I cannot reveal to anyone the secrets of life and death, nor do I ask anyone to believe what I believe. I keep my personal religious beliefs entirely separate from my work as a clairvoyant.

Being psychic does not necessarily give you any deeper insight into the origins of your gift than other people. Obviously it does not; otherwise all psychically gifted people would proclaim the same answer, which is not the case. Christian psychics claim they speak with Christ; Moslems receive their messages from Mohammed; Buddhists meet with Buddha, and so on, and each claims to have tapped the mainspring of human existence. They can't all be right. And when one of these "mystic" psychics makes a pronouncement that is proved wrong—how can this be? Does God make mistakes?

In the same way, I dissociate myself completely from all forms of superstition, and especially those related to what is called "the occult." To me this term implies that if you believe in ESP and psychic phenomena, you must also subscribe to some arcane superstition or mumbo jumbo. At the least, you must be some kind of gullible person, easily taken in by hocus-pocus.

No, I reject all schools of thought that associate ESP with religion, philosophy, or superstition. They oversimplify a complex question, they distort, they leave the way open for cruel exploitation of the weak and the insecure by charlatans and frauds, and too often they smack of shrewd opportunism. For too long the field of ESP has been clouded with dogma and mysticism and "black" practices. One of my prime hopes for this book is that it will help blow this kind of obscurantist thinking out the window.

At the same time, I do not use any "method." I am not an astrologer, nor do I cast cards or read tea leaves or gaze into a crystal ball. I do use my divining rod, but I have already explained that it is an aid to me and has no powers of its own.

This is not to say, however, that I consider all astrologers, or all the proponents of "mystic ESP" frauds or crooks. It is entirely possible that some of these people can generate their own ESP by using objects or concentrating on a particular thing, even if it is a belief, or a deity in whom they have been taught to believe.

I do believe, however, that ESP is a *human* faculty. It exists within the individual's mind. Its energies may be tapped by the individual in various ways, but it is there within the mind, and my main argument against "mystic" or "occult" attitudes toward ESP is that they contribute nothing to our deeper understanding of this situation.

My concern, as I said, is for parapsychology—but again, for a long time and particularly since my arrival in the United States, I have been concerned that much of what is being done now in the field of parapsychological research will contribute little more to our deeper understanding of ourselves than mystic attitudes have in the past.

I hope to go into this more deeply later, when we discuss some of my experiences with scientific researchers, but I believe that much of what is being done now is leading us down blind alleys, toward conclusions that will prove unsatisfactory and even misleading.

The main problem is that many researchers have taken an overly academic and scientific approach to what is essentially a *human* question. The psychic gift exists somewhere in the human psyche, buried in the subconscious, and it is within the human mind that we should be seeking it.

This is the reason I have taken such pains to explain the problems that beset me in my youth. It worries me that there may be children in the world right now who are lost in the same harrowing confusion in which I was trapped for so many years, and that the people who should be investigating their problems—the parapsychologists—may not even be aware that the problems exist. The scientists themselves may be lost among their graphs and statistics.

A psychic gift, far from being some minor ability useful for identifying cards and playing party games in laboratories, can be a powerful force in the human mind. Unless the individual learns to control it in time—as I did, but not without help, guidance, luck, and a great deal of effort—it can be destructive to that individual's own life and peace of mind. I know this from bitter experience, but many parapsychologists seem to ignore even the possibility.

Unfortunately, by treating ESP as a minor ability, they have also ignored the fact that psychic talents can be enormously useful when applied to problems in the real world—not statistical problems, not party-game problems, not questions of "which-card-is-this" or "which-light-will-come-on-next," but real, practical, *human* problems.

My prime purpose in writing this book is to demonstrate that psychic abilities are real and can be extremely useful in the real world. Accordingly, from now on I ask you to believe nothing. If you have any preconceived notions about what ESP is and what can be done with it, forget them. I ask you merely to examine the evidence, and decide for yourself whether or not ESP is useful. I stand, and my gift stands, on what I have accomplished.

The legend of the Host of Niervaart comes from the archives of the Dutch town of Breda, not far from the Belgian border, and from the history of the Roman Catholic Church. It tells us that early in the thirteenth century a peasant farmer named Jan Bautoen, digging for peat near the now-destroyed township of Niervaart in the Dutch lowlands, uncovered what appeared to be a Host. (A Host by the Catholic definition is a small wafer consecrated in the Eucharist, representing the body of Christ.)

This Host was apparently intact, and Jan Bautoen took it to the priest in Niervaart, who installed it in his church and notified the bishop of Liege. The bishop sent a representative with instructions to test the Host with three strokes of his dagger, in the name of the Father, Son, and Holy Ghost.

On the third stroke of the dagger, according to the legend, blood poured from the host and the priest's arm became paralyzed.

The Host was immediately deemed to be divine. Miraculous healing powers were claimed for it. Niervaart became a destination for pilgrims as revered as Lourdes and Czestochowa are today.

But the journey to Niervaart was not an easy one. The lowlands were subject to frequent and serious floods. In 1449 the Host was moved to the more accessible town of Breda, where it was installed in the already ancient church. Breda became a prosperous city because of the large amount of pilgrim traffic.

Then, in 1566, during the war between Dutch Catholics and Protestants—the so-called Three Days of Iconoclasm—the Host vanished. During the struggle Protestant forces overran Breda, and it was thought that in their orgy of destruction of Catholic churches and chattels, they may have burned the ancient relic.

A more acceptable theory to Catholics, however, was that one of the priests had hidden or buried it, probably hoping to recover it after the war. Almost certainly, no relic of such significance would have been surrendered too readily to the iconoclasts, nor would any priest have destroyed it.

The church in Breda became Protestant and it remains so today. It is known as the Onze Lieve Vrouwe Church, and its 320-foot spire—which took 150 years to build—casts a peaceful shadow over the center of the town.

It was the Onze Lieve Vrouwe Church, along with other historic buildings in the old town, that attracted me to Breda in December, 1948. I hoped that by looking into the "lives" of the old buildings I might find a project as intriguing as the assassination of Willem in the Prinsenhof. As I was neither a Catholic nor a *Bredanaar* nor a student of church history I had never heard of the Host of Niervaart—indeed, I would not have known a Host if I had seen one. I was interested in the church, the building itself.

Breda is only thirty-five miles from Rotterdam, so I took a train, planning to return the same evening.

In the church I found my way down to the tombs where heavy marble slabs covered the burial places of priests and church dignitaries dating back to the time of the Iconoclasm and earlier. This seemed a likely place to start, so I took out my divining rod and concentrated on one of the sarcophagi. I wanted to know if it actually contained human remains. It did.

While I was standing there, a priest approached and asked what I was doing.

"I'm looking inside," I told him. "I am clairvoyant and I'm trying to find out if there is really a body in there. You'll be happy to know there is."

He smiled noncommittally, but said nothing.

I asked him where I could learn some history of the church, and he directed me to the Breda mayoral chambers where the town's archives were kept.

I went to the town hall, and when the clerk came to assist me I told him my story. "I'm interested in the history of the Onze Lieve Vrouwe Church," I said. "I am psychic and I'd like to investigate some historical story, some event that is believed to have taken place in the church."

As I said this, another clerk overheard and he came to the counter. "You are psychic?" he asked.

"I am."

"Then I have a case for you," he said, and he told me the legend of the Host of Niervaart. "Most people think it was buried somewhere in the town and that it might still be found. Perhaps you can find it."

I told him I didn't know, but I was willing to try anything. Eventually we agreed to meet on the steps of the church later in the afternoon, after he and the other clerk finished work.

To fill in time I went to another Catholic church and asked the priest there to show me a Host. I had no idea what I was going to be looking for, and I wanted to get it straight in my own mind before I started.

The priest produced a thin wafer, and the moment I saw it I *knew* the object I was seeking existed. Somewhere in this town of ninety thousand people one of these Hosts was buried, and I was sure my gift would lead me to it.

I told the priest so, and he was amused but polite. It would be a wonderful thing for the church, he said, if the Host could be found, and although he could not offer any official assistance, he asked to be kept informed of developments.

His name, incidentally, was Chaplain de Vet. He was later to help me during my own conversion to Catholicism, and later still to become bishop of Breda.

At five-thirty in the afternoon I met the two clerks, whose names were Mallee and Berbers, on the steps of the old church. In the meantime, they had advised the mayor and the archivist of the proposed search by clairvoyance and these officials, too, asked to be kept informed. Mallee had brought along a clipboard and a map of the town.

I had no idea *how* I was going to conduct this search, so I simply took out my divining rod and concentrated on the ancient missing Host. Almost immediately I felt a strange sensation grip me. It's beyond my power to describe it, but it was a physical as well as a mental sensation, my gift was being unleashed inside me with all its power.

It began with a sense of disorientation, of dizziness, almost of nausea, that suddenly congealed into physical pain that took my breath away. It was like an electric shock—suddenly every joint, every muscle ached. I hunched forward, almost fell, and could not straighten up. In my mind I saw *beyond* reality. I remained aware of my surroundings—Mallee and Berbers, the modern buildings, the traffic, passersby—but I could also "see" a different town! Different streets, old buildings, unpaved, narrow, haphazard streets and lanes. . . . Breda as it had been sometime in the past!

Then in my mind I saw a priest. Very old, bent, stooped, arthritic, crippled. He stood before us and was as real to me as Mallee and Berbers. In his arms he held an old metal box, a chest, perhaps two-by-one-by-one-foot deep. Then he began walking away, hobbling, shuffling, limping along one of those old lanes with his crippled gait.

I followed, shuffling as he shuffled, bent and pain-wracked as he was—and ran straight into a stone wall! I stopped, let go the wire. The old priest disappeared. I went around the wall and took up the wire again. And he was there, shuffling along, leading me.

It took hours. The old priest led the way, never looking back, along streets and alleyways that were not there. Many times I bumped into walls and buildings and had to go around them, and the old priest was always there on the other side, hobbling along in front of me, holding the box in his arms.

From the Onze Lieve Vrouwe Church we went in a wide, roughly circular route as far as the bank of a canal, then along the canal for about a mile before doubling back and circling again until we found ourselves on the doorstep of a shoemaker's shop directly across the street from our starting point—the old church.

"I have to go inside," I said. "It is here."

The shoemaker's name was Opperman. After some discussion, he allowed us to go inside. Still the old priest led me, through the house and down into the cellar. In the middle of the floor he vanished. I knew I had come to the place.

"It is here," I said. "Underneath the floor there is a metal box. Very old. It is buried right here, beneath my feet!"

At this point Mallee and Berbers became very excited. What kind of box? they wanted to know. What was inside it?

I concentrated on the box. The cellar floor consisted of stone slabs, or tiles. Holding the divining rod in my hands, I moved very slowly across the floor until I got a reaction from the leading edge of the box beneath the floor.

"Mister Opperman," I said to the shoemaker, "please get some chalk and make a line on the floor—right here."

He did. Then, still relying on my instinctive reactions from the divining rod, I moved my hands forward until I got a reaction from the far edge of the box. Opperman drew a line there. I moved along these lines in the same way, until we had on the floor lines showing the exact dimensions of the box buried below. It was almost exactly eighteen inches long by fourteen inches wide.

Then I concentrated on the contents, using the same method of "drawing" the outlines with the tip of the loop of my divining rod. At the same time I could "see" in my mind what the box contained.

When I had finished, the chalk drawing on the stone floor described a circle about one foot in diameter. A narrow band ran from this circle, then expanded again into a flat piece at the end. At the center of the big circle was another, smaller circle, about two inches in diameter.

Mallee and Berbers were dismayed. "But that's a monstrance!" they cried.

"I don't know what a monstrance is," I said. "But this thing stands upright on this flat base. I don't understand it, but it contains some old cloth and pieces of human bone, and gold and silver, and in the small circle at the center there is a Host."

The next morning at the town hall I found everyone in a rare state of excitement, for Mallee had come up with a remarkable discovery. On his map the day before he had charted the route I had taken on my psychic walk through the town. Because I had kept bumping into buildings and having to go around them in order to "follow" the old priest, my path bore little relation to the plan of the modern town.

But when they overlaid my route on a map of the town as it had been at the time of the Iconoclasm—the year 1566—they discovered that my walk would have taken me through the streets of the town exactly as it was then—four hundred years earlier!

Furthermore, from the Onze Lieve Vrouwe Church the walk would have taken me to Spaanse Gat, Markendaalsweg, Haagdijk, and The Haven—all exit points in those days. It appeared that the old priest had tried to flee the town with his precious relics. But he had found all the gates under attack, and finally had gone back to bury his metal box in a safe place.

Mallee and Berbers had learned from the archives that Josef Opperman's shop had once been an outbuilding of the church. In the sixteenth century it had been the home of the sexton—a logical place for a priest to have buried precious relics.

By this time, the mayor of Breda, a Mr. Prinsen, had been informed of developments in the search and was very enthusiastic. The city would help in any way it could, he said. What a thing it would be for Breda if the sacred Host was recovered!

In the meantime, Mallee and Berbers had found a sponsor willing to finance a digging operation in the cellar and compensate the shoemaker Opperman for any damage. At first I was opposed to involving commercial interests in the search, but when I met the sponsor, an automobile dealer named Pieter Otten, I gave way to the idea. Pieter Otten was genuinely concerned for the recovery of the Host, and we later became firm friends.

The Opperman family also treated me very kindly, and after so many years alone I began to feel that I had finally found a home in Breda.

Later that morning, in the cellar, I met a priest named Rector Huysman.

"I am an expert in the history of the sacred Host of Niervaart," he told me. "I would like to ask you some questions about this box."

"Go ahead," I said. "But I have to tell you, I am not a Catholic. My interest in the case is purely parapsychological. The religious side of it means nothing to me."

He asked me what was in the box, and I repeated what I had said the day before. The box contained a monstrance: gold, silver, cloth, pieces of human bone, and a Host.

"I don't believe you," he said.

"Well," I replied. "I'm sorry, but I don't care about that."

"Tell me about the Host," he said. "Are there, for instance, any holes in it?"

I took out the divining rod and concentrated on the Host. "Yes," I said. "There are three holes in it."

"This is too much!" he cried. "You are reading my mind!"

"I'm not," I said. "I just looked inside the box, that's all."

Now he became very quiet. "Church history tells us," he said, "that when the Host was taken to Niervaart, the bishop of Liege sent an emissary to test its miraculous powers. This priest took a dagger and stabbed the Host three times, in the name of the Father, the Son, and the Holy Ghost. At the third stroke of the dagger, blood flowed from the Host. Do you believe that?"

"Why not?" I replied. "I know there is more to life than we understand. I don't even understand what I do, myself."

"You must have been reading my mind," he insisted, "to know about the three holes in the sacred Host!"

"I'm sorry," I said, "but I don't read minds. I see the Host, that's all."

Later still, an engineer arrived to determine how the box might be raised.

"We are going to have a problem," he said. "All this area is undermined with quicksand. Tell me, is the box directly beneath this drawing on the floor?"

"Yes," I said.

"All right. We will take up the tiles and dig. When we break through to quicksand we will put a concrete cylinder down around the box. Underground pressure will force the mud to rise in the cylinder, and the box will come with it."

Immediately I sensed that something was wrong with his plan, and I consulted my gift about it.

"No," I said. "Listen, it won't work. The box is in quicksand, but you will have to put pipes down around it to dry out the mud, then bring it up with hooks and ropes. If you put a heavy concrete cylinder down, the box will shift away in the mud and you will lose it."

But I was ignored. The next day workmen tore up the tiles and dug into the foundations. The composition of the foundations was important to the case. They consisted of rye meal mixed with clay to make a kind of mortar that had not been used for hundreds of years. The foundations of the shoemaker's shop had not been disturbed in centuries.

Two or three feet down, the picks broke through to quicksand, which quickly began to rise in the hole. I leaped forward with a pole and probed in the mud. At a depth of about six feet I made contact with something solid. Something solid and rectangular in shape. Something metallic and hollow. A metal box.

At this point everyone became excited again. The foundations had not been disturbed for hundreds of years. Below them, just as I had said, was a metal box.

A notary was called to witness the raising of the box and its opening, so there could be no argument over the genuineness of its contents.

But then, against my advice, the excavators brought in an enormous concrete cylinder, at least three feet in diameter, with walls three inches thick.

"Listen," I said again, "if you push that down in the mud, the box will shift away. You will lose it."

Again I was ignored. Electronic soundings were taken, and they confirmed that the object in the mud was rectangular and metallic. But nothing would persuade them to put stakes around the box to prevent it from moving.

The cylinder went down. Mud rose in it—but not the box. More soundings were taken. The metal box had moved away in the mud. It was now either under the wall of the building, or further out, under the street.

I was enraged, and tremendously disappointed. I had located the box, and it was there. But when it came to bringing it out of the mud, my advice had been ignored.

For a long time confusion reigned, giving way to angry recriminations. If the box was to be recovered now, the street would have to be torn up or the old building at least partly demolished. The expense would be enormous. To make matters worse, the experts estimated that a major excavation so close to the Onze Lieve Vrouwe Church across the street might lead to the weakening of its ancient foundations. It, too, was undermined with quicksand, and any drastic shifting of the mud might bring its beautiful spire crashing down.

The technical problems of raising the box now were formidable, and neither the city nor the sponsor could afford to risk such an undertaking. The arguments raged for days, then for weeks, before the project was finally shelved indefinitely.

Naturally I was disappointed by the failure of the excavators to raise the box after I had found it, but I was even more dismayed when people began to say that I had promised to recover the sacred Host of Niervaart but had failed to deliver the goods.

Throughout the search, I was not concerned with the religious aspects. To me it was just another case, an experiment for my gift. I knew that the floor under the cellar contained a monstrance and a Host, but since I was not a Catholic or even a religious man of any kind, these objects themselves were unimportant to me. I was more concerned with using my psychic abilities as fully as possible.

However, as the case went on and I learned more about the Host itself, and as I became more involved with priests and other devout Catholics I had met, I began to think more and more about my personal beliefs.

I had set out to search for the so-called "sacred Host," and my gift had led me to it. I was convinced that it existed. It was there, in the box.

From this moment I began to change my personal philosophy and eventually, as I have already indicated, I converted to Catholicism. Without wishing to impress my own beliefs on anyone, I can say that my conversion was brought about largely by things I learned during my search for the Host of Niervaart.

One other aspect of the case should be mentioned. Under Dutch law, Josef Opperman and I were entitled to claim part ownership of whatever was contained in the metal box I had located beneath the cellar floor. But we knew that it contained religious relics, and that these relics were extremely valuable to the Catholic Church. We wanted no profit from them, nor did we want to allow anyone else to profit from my work by withholding these relics from the Church.

Accordingly, in cooperation with the sponsor Pieter Otten and the clerks, Mallee and Berbers, the shoemaker Josef Opperman and I hired a lawyer, Dr. Van Schayk, of Maarsen, Utrecht, to draw up a contract covering the contents of the metal box.

Under the terms of this contract, both Opperman and I relinquished our claims to the contents in favor of the bishop of Breda, who was at that time Bishop Baeten.

This contract still applies—and the box is still there, either beneath the building or under the street. I know it, and when I return to Europe in the near future, I believe that I will be able to find it again—and this time we will bring it up.

5

THE CLAIRVOYANT OF BREDA

While a final decision on whether or not to raise the metal box remained in abeyance with the local authorities, I stayed on in Breda. I moved from my hotel room to a small apartment and started giving consultations. My first clients were people I had met since arriving in the town, but before long the publicity over the search for the Host of Niervaart brought so many people to my office that it became apparent I would have to stay in Breda for some time.

I remained for twelve years. Breda became my home and base and I became known, after the European custom of identifying a man by his place of residence, as "Dykshoorn of Breda."

For the most part 1949 was a year of consolidation, trial, and experimentation. I realized that if I was to survive as a professional clairvoyant I would need to build up a list of regular clients who would come back for consultations over long periods of time. It was not enough merely to demonstrate ESP; I was determined that my work would be useful and valuable, so from the beginning I tried to give each client far more than a basic "reading."

If my client had a specific problem, I would try to determine how my gift could help in particular ways. Only by doing this could I extend the range and scope of my work and find out what I was capable of accomplishing—and very often I startled myself as much as my client.

In water-divining, for example, I found that I was able to refine the basic technique quite considerably. I had been diverted from my plans in this field in Rotterdam, but in Breda I took it up again. Farmers asked me to dowse for water on their properties and at first I would go along and walk in their fields, waiting for a reaction from my gift to tell me I was over a water source.

But I discovered that I could usually locate so many water sources that the farmer was left with a choice, so then I would try to help him choose. I would ask myself: "At what depth is the water here? Can it be used for livestock only, or irrigation only, or both?" Happily, I found I could get reliable answers from my gift. From there it was only a short step to the stage where I would decide before I started dowsing what kind of water I would try to find, and at what depth I would try to find it.

One day a farmer visited me in my office in town and asked me to find water on his property. Because I didn't have the time to go with him, I asked him to draw a rough, freehand map of his farm on a piece of paper and I went over that with the divining rod, "dowsing" on the paper instead of the actual farmland. I learned that the loop would react to a certain point on the map, giving a true indication of where water could be found. Later, by counting distances off inside my head, I could pinpoint the exact spot at which the farmer should put down his well—without ever leaving my office.

This is known as "map-dowsing," and although only a small proportion of my clients came to me for dowsing work, I found it a very useful ability, especially since—as I had proved by finding the old bricks in Delft—it could be used to locate things older than water.

Within a matter of months, in fact, I would employ it to locate human remains, but before that I worked on another case in which my results were witnessed and documented by impartial and unimpeachable observers.

On October 10, 1949, a man named Willem van Aartsen telephoned me from Middelburg. He told me that he was a water-diviner, but he now found himself confronted with a task beyond his dowsing ability. He wondered if I could help.

It seemed that van Aartsen had been asked by a friend of his, one Anton Touburg, to locate a cache of money that had been buried in the garden of a house in Middelburg by Toubourg's deceased brother-in-law. The brother-in-law, named Jan Meijboom, had died in Lisse the previous December, but before moving to Lisse he had lived in Middelburg at Seisstraat, Number 28. He had been forced to evacuate this address during the war, but before leaving he had buried in the garden a package containing three hundred rixdollars. (The rixdollar was an old denomination of Dutch currency which became obsolete after the Second World War. Its value was two and one half guilders, or approximately one U.S. dollar.)

After Meijboom's death it was learned that he had named his sister Johanna, Touburg's wife, as his sole heiress. As far as anyone knew, the hoard he had buried in the garden of his Middelburg home had never been recovered, and no one knew exactly where it was hidden. The house had since been taken by another family, but they denied having found any cash.

Touburg's wife could claim the money if it was found, but obviously Touburg could not go digging up the entire garden of a house owned by another family. So he had asked van Aartsen to look for the money, but van Aartsen had had no success.

I agreed to go down to Middelburg and look for the money, and the next morning, October 11, I went down by train.

Van Aartsen met me at the station. "If you don't mind," he said, "we've asked a notary public to come along and witness the search. If you find the money, we don't want any dispute about who found it, or where."

"That's fine with me," I said. "I don't know whether I can find it or not, but I'm willing to try."

We went on to the office of the notary public, Robert Batten. I had expected to find him skeptical about the proposed search, but he said: "I heard about what you did in Breda last year, and I'm not about to make a fool of myself by saying you can't do it here. But I warn you, I will record only what I see. Nothing more."

"Good," I said. "I'm a clairvoyant. I only tell what I see, too. Nothing more."

Then the three of us, accompanied by one of Batten's clerks, Jan Lakerveld, went down to the house at Seisstraat, 28. The lady of the house let us inside, but she was more than a little dubious about the whole thing.

"There's nothing there," she said. "You think we could live here for five years and not find money in the garden?"

"May we dig if we have to, Madam?" I asked.

"Oh, you're welcome," she said. "But don't go digging up the whole place. There's nothing there, anyway."

I took out my divining rod and concentrated on the man who had last seen the money, the man who had buried it—Jan Meijboom. Immediately "he," or some force related to him as he had been, even though he had died a year earlier, came into me. Following the procedure I had adopted in Breda when I concentrated on the old priest, I hunched into a stoop and began shuffling forward. And I saw the old man, his neck askew, one arm twisted, leading me out into the garden.

It took less than a minute. The old man led me straight down the garden about ten yards, then he stopped and vanished.

"It is here," I said. "It's right under my feet. Please dig."

Van Aartsen dug, and less than a foot deep in the soil his spade struck a cache of loose, unwrapped bundles of blackened silver coins. They had evidently been wrapped in newspaper when buried years before, but the paper had rotted away and the coins now lay loose in the soil.

They were counted on the spot, and they totaled exactly three hundred rixdollars.

Back in his office the notary, Robert Batten, prepared a statement documenting and verifying what had taken place at the house, and the declaration was signed by himself, van Aartsen, and the clerk Lakerveld. I still have the original of this affidavit, and a certified translation. (See Appendix.)

Antwerp, in Belgium, is just across the border from Breda and is, in fact, the nearest big city to that Dutch town. *Bredanaars* spend a good deal of time in Antwerp, and in those day I was no exception. I had many friends in Antwerp, and went there often.

One day in early 1950, some of my friends from Antwerp let me know that the police in that city "would not reject" an offer of assistance in their investigation of a particularly tragic and frightening case. Three weeks earlier a young girl had left her home in that city to go to school and had never returned. A friend had seen her on a street corner after school, but after that she had simply disappeared without a trace. She was twelve years old.

The request, of course, was oblique. The police did not want it known they were seeking the help of a clairvoyant. Later, after I had worked many times for the police forces not only of Belgium but of Holland, West Germany, and Luxembourg as well and had established bases of mutual trust with them, the requests came more directly. For the moment, however, the onus was on me to offer my services. Naturally, I went to Antwerp and spoke with the Inspector of Police.

He was very frank. "Mister Dykshoorn," he said, "we welcome your assistance, and we hope you can help. But I must ask you not to talk about this with anyone, and least of all the newspapers. In fact, we're going to swear you in as a special deputy. If you try to capitalize on your involvement in this case, you will be liable for prosecution. And you will never work for the police again, anywhere. Do you understand?"

I understood. He could hardly have stated it more clearly.

We went to the street corner where the child had last been seen. I took out my divining wire and concentrated on her. Immediately I was assailed by the familiar physical sensation. This time, however, the feeling was the most violent I had ever experienced. I choked, and could not breath. I fell to my knees and actually vomited on the ground.

I knew then. "I am sorry," I said, "but the girl is dead. Strangled. A man strangled her, and then I think he threw her into a canal. He dragged her into his car and took her away. I can describe the man, and the car, but first I would like to find the girl."

Antwerp is crisscrossed with canals. The inspector brought me a detailed map of the city and I worked over it with the divining rod. It indicated a specific place and we went there together.

The canal was wide and murky and steadily flowing. I walked along the bank until I knew I was standing at the exact spot from which the man had thrown the girl's body into the water.

"This is the place," I said. "He threw her into the water from exactly this spot. The body has been carried some distance downstream by the current, but it is there. You will find it in about two weeks."

Then I described the man I had seen in my mind, and his car, and went home to Breda.

Exactly fourteen days later the police recovered the body of the child. It was about one hundred meters downstream from the spot on which I had stood. She had not drowned, but had been thrown into the water after death. She had been strangled.

As I had promised, I said nothing to the press about the case, but too many people had known about it and the story found its way into the newspapers of Holland and Belgium. For a while I was worried that the police might think I had abused their trust, but to my amazement I learned that, far from keeping quiet about

it themselves, they had opened their files on the case to the reporters!

The following is extracted from the Belgian newspaper *Het
Handelsblad,* of March 21, 1950, and *Dagblad de Stem* (Breda)
of March 20, 1950:

> In the case of [girl's name] we have therefore seen a
> striking testimonial. It seems that Dykshoorn was correct in
> every respect. He stated to the police that the girl had been
> strangled and thrown into the canal. The body was found
> only 100 meters downstream, presumably having been taken
> there by the current.
>
> A statement prepared by the police a month [sic] before
> stands to prove that there is no possibility of deception. This
> statement will remove the aura of the unbelievable from
> Mr. Dykshoorn, because of the proportion of his predictions
> that came to reality.

6

BODIES IN THE WATER

I don't boast about it, but I think I am the only psychic ever to have physically located human remains. I have seen a great deal of pain and unpleasantness in my life, both in my personal reality and in the various realities to which I have had access through my gift, but none compares with the awful moment when you know a child has died and you have to try and find the body. Such a moment has to be endured, and such a task has to be treated as a job; to dwell on such things can only be self-destructive.

Between 1950 and 1960 I worked more than twenty times for and in cooperation with the police forces of Holland, Belgium, West Germany, and Luxembourg, usually on cases of disappearance, kidnapping, or murder, and always in secrecy. Very few of these cases were reported in the press. As was the situation in Antwerp I was almost invariably sworn in as a special deputy or "expert adviser" to the police, and I believe it was only because of my willingness to work in confidence that the police allowed me to become involved in these cases.

For this reason, and because I hope to be able to work for the police in the United States, as I have already done several times,

I will relate here only those cases that became public knowledge at the time and for which I have documented evidence of my accomplishments. For the rest, the reader will have to believe that a few represent the many, and that the results I achieved in the reported cases were duplicated many times in other situations.

If anyone remains doubtful and wishes to conduct further research, my record is on file with the Netherlands Department of Justice in The Hague. In any event, I believe that my work in this area led to my claim to psychic abilities being endorsed by the Dutch government when I was issued a passport listing my occupation as *helderziende*—"clairvoyant." As far as I know, I am the only psychic ever to have been so honored.

In June of 1951 I received a telephone call for assistance from an alderman in the town of Sluis, a picturesque little town in the southwestern corner of Holland not far from the coast and just inside the border with Belgium.

An old man, an inmate of a home for the elderly in Sluis, had disappeared. Several days earlier he had left his room and set out to walk into the town, but he had never returned.

By this time I had bought myself a small motorcycle, so I set out to ride the ninety miles from Breda to Sluis. I went directly to the town hall and sought out the alderman, who introduced me to the mayor. The mayor, in turn, called for the manager of the home and we went into conference.

In the mayor's office I took out the divining rod and concentrated on the old man. I soon began to choke and splutter, and my throat seemed to fill with water. I knew, then, the old man had drowned.

We went to the home, to the old man's room, and I set out to follow the course he had taken on his last walk. My gift brought him into me: I shuffled, my right eye twitched, I felt again the familiar sensation of pain that was not my own.

The manager was astonished. "That's him!" he cried. "That's exactly the way he walked. You are him!"

The room was one of many opening into a long, narrow hallway. At each door I felt a compulsion to stoop and peer through the keyhole. "The old man was a peeping tom," I said. "He liked to look through the keyholes. You had to speak to him about it."

"Yes," the manager said, weakly.

"He was not really very old," I said. "He was only about fifty. But he was retarded and an unhealthy attachment to his mother left him unable to cope with the world. That was why he was admitted here in the first place. Then a couple of weeks ago you told him his mother had died, and the news broke him. He brooded over it for a few days, and then he disappeared."

"This is beyond me!" the manager said. "But it is all true. That is his history!"

As before, the old man was there. I saw him and felt that I *was* he. Following him, I went into the town and into a church where he had prayed, then from the church to a tavern, then from the tavern to the bank of the canal that winds its peaceful way through the town.

There I stopped. It was different now. The old man in my mind had led me to this point, which was the point from which he had jumped into the water. He could not lead me farther.

It was at this stage that I had ended my search for the drowned girl in Antwerp, telling the police that the body was somewhere close by in the water. Now I felt that I could do more; I had a strong urge to carry on, to search for the body itself here and now. My gift said yes, the body was there.

"Bring the police," I said. "The body is there now, in the water. It has never floated to the surface because it is tangled in the branches of a tree embedded in the mud. But it is there and we will find it."

The mayor summoned the police and they arrived in less than ten minutes with grappling hooks and nets. They were accompanied by a reporter from the local newspaper.

A small boat was requisitioned and the policemen and I rowed out into the canal. I was dowsing now, searching with the divining rod, waiting for the indication that we were directly over the body.

It came. "Here," I said.

The police lowered their hooks into the water, struck something solid, hooked and heaved. Their first heave brought the body to the surface.

Everyone present—myself excluded—was profoundly shocked. No one had expected actually to find the body, but here it was.

Suddenly, amid the confusion, a macabre and rather farcical argument started. It seemed that the spot at which I had found the body was about fifty yards across the border and was actually in Belgium—this being the canal connecting Sluis with Bruges— and to have moved the body back across the border would have been tantamount to smuggling!

I suggested we should lower it back into the water and tow it back to Holland, but the police would not condone that maneuver. Finally, the Belgian police were called and the body had to be taken to Bruges, only to be returned later to Sluis for burial.

A coroner's enquiry later returned a verdict of death by drowning, exact circumstances unknown, and the following story appeared in *Ad Vertentieblad,* June 8, 1951. Because of the sad nature of the old man's disappearance and death, it reported only the barest details.

> A —— from the —— Home, disappeared several days ago and was believed to have met with an accident. Police investigated in cooperation with the diviner Dykshoorn of Breda. This brought them to dragging in the canal between Sluis and Bruges, where the body was found. Because it was within Belgian territory the body was taken to Bruges and later returned to Sluis.

The next case was even more tragic than the two I have already described, yet I relate it because in one way it was the most important case of that period of my life. It marked another turning point in my attitude toward myself and my gift.

I have already said, in an earlier chapter, that I disagree with some of the lines of research currently being followed by para-psychologists because they seem to be trying to attribute ESP to mechanistic rather than human causes. I hope to go into this more deeply later, but for the moment I can say that my conviction was born out of experience, and out of one particular experience I had in 1952.

It was Tuesday, February 12, in the afternoon. I was undergoing tests at a Dutch provincial university that shall remain nameless here. I had volunteered for the tests, as I had volunteered for others, in the hope of perhaps gaining some answer to the puzzling and important question thrown up by the fact of my gift's existence. But even then I had often been disappointed by some of the methods used by the researchers.

Most of the researchers I encountered in Europe impressed me very much. Several of them accompanied me on murder cases and I was grateful for their open-mindedness and dedication to careful, thorough investigation of psychic phenomena. But others annoyed me equally as much.

These were the men who seemed determined to prove that psychic abilities should relate to inanimate objects—lights, cards with symbols printed on them, words concealed in envelopes, black and white marbles, and all the other paraphernalia of statistical testing—rather then to people. Their tests always took place in their laboratories, never in the real world of human activity.

Like others, I submitted to these statistical tests in which the probabilities were worked out in advance by the researchers, who were prepared to say that if you could not identify symbolic cards up to the levels of their preconceptions, you did not possess ESP. Over the months I had submitted with increasing reluctance and resentment. I knew what I had done, and the press, the public, the police, the government, and even the researchers themselves knew what I had done, but they insisted the games-playing should continue. The statistics had to be compiled, the graphs completed. Twenty percent was an "average" score; 40 percent "good"; 60 percent "excellent"; 80 percent "remarkable." Pick the next card, please. Tell me which light will come on next, sparked by the random switch.

I would not have minded if these tests had been preliminary, part of a careful program to investigate all the possibilities of ESP. I knew what they were seeking: They were trying to prove that all human beings possess some extrasensory ability to a greater or lesser extent, by testing a great number of people and tabulating their results against the norm. Some people have it, some don't— but what was *it*? As I say, I would not have minded being subjected to five-minute tests of this type, as part of the program.

But I had been invited to participate in the research because I was known to be psychic. They knew what I had done and did not contest my work or the results I had achieved. They had asked me here, they claimed, to find out *how* I did what I did, which was exactly what I wanted to know. But now that I was here, it was games-playing all the way. Not for minutes or even hours, but for *days* on end. And it was obvious that this was the *only* way they intended to test my abilities. There would be no tests on people, but only on these dumb, dead, inanimate objects.

At one point I tried to argue. "Send someone into town and tell him to bring back fifty people off the street," I said. "I will tell them all about themselves, past, present, and future. Work out the graphs on *that* data, because *that* is what my gift is all about!"

"Pick the next card, please," they replied.

As the days wore on, my anger thickened into disgust. The tests were long, tedious, and boring. I was tired and my concentration was beginning to lapse.

To make matters worse, these particular tests were studded with tricks and loaded questions—calculated, cynical traps designed to make the subject err, or appear to err. There were questions to which there were no correct answers. For example: A deck of cards was supposed to consist of cards with different symbols on the faces—square, circle, triangle, wavy lines. I ask my gift: Square? Circle? Triangle? Waves? I get a reaction, and I answer. I don't see the symbol in my mind because I have no person I can relate to. Ring in a card with a new symbol. Vertical lines. I ask my gift: Square? Circle? Triangle? Waves? No reaction. So I answer: "I don't know." Wrong answer.

I try to explain that in this type of test I have to ask my gift direct questions, yes–no questions. I can't see the card because there is no person involved. Wrong answer recorded on the graph. Pick the next card, please. I start to think about the clients I have kept waiting while I submit to this procedure.

Then, that February 12, 1952, the researchers went too far. They introduced a test in which I was required to state whether smears of blood on glass slides came from a man or a woman.

At first I was encouraged by this test. At least the blood came from human subjects; I could tell them my psychic impressions of the people.

But they cut me short. The question was: Man or woman? No further information was required, or even noted down when supplied.

Then they set down in front of me a sample of blood from which I received a very strange psychic impression. At first I was surprised, then enraged.

I stood up. "Gentlemen," I said, "thank you for inviting me here, but I do not wish to participate further in the program. I am very tired and simply cannot be bothered wasting my time avoiding childish traps. You are playing games with a very serious subject, and I deeply resent the implication that I am merely a fraud who has never been exposed. My abilities and the way I use them are public knowledge, and until you can disprove my abilities, please do not degrade them. This blood sample has been taken from a female. A pregnant female. A pregnant female dog—or maybe a fox; I don't know. Now, if you will excuse me. . . ."

I walked out of the university and went home. My phone was ringing as I entered my apartment. Two children had disappeared in Tilburg, about fifteen miles away. This man's daughter, and the daughter of a neighbor. Both girls were three years old.

Half an hour later the man picked me up and we set out for

Tilburg in his car. On the way, I worked it out, endured the awful moments.

We went to the police station and then to the banks of the Wilhelmina Canal. My gift led me to the exact spot from which the children had fallen into the water and then, immediately, to the body of the first child. There had been no foul play. One child had fallen into the water, the other had tried to help her, but the first girl had struggled too vigorously and dragged the second girl into the canal.

A few minutes later the police recovered the second tiny body.

I could not boast about the parapsychological significance of what my gift had enabled me to do, but I learned an important lesson that afternoon. I knew my own gift better than anyone, and perhaps better than anyone ever would. Probably I would never achieve a full understanding of it. It had been granted me, for whatever reason, by the forces that control human destinies, perhaps by the life force itself, whatever it is, and like this force itself it might remain forever beyond explanation and beyond my understanding.

Yet it worked. Beyond doubt, it worked. And I would use it because ultimately, now as before, I had no choice except to use it. The researchers and statisticians could play their simple games, but I would never excuse myself because my gift did not fit into their patterns or dovetail with their theories. I would simply use it whenever and wherever I could—according to my own lights and my own unfathomable destiny.

There was, incidentally, an ironic postscript to the story of my dealings with the university parapsychologists. The next morning, February 13, one of the researchers phoned—to apologize.

He had read in the newspaper about my help in finding and recovering the children's bodies, so he wanted to apologize in a general way, but he also had a smaller apology to add.

They had not been aware that all the blood samples were not human. In fact, they had been as surprised as I had been by my curious psychic impression. But he had traced the samples back to their source, he said, and had learned that a laboratory assistant, knowing the slides were to be used to test "phony clairvoyants," had taken blood from a fox and slipped it in among the human samples.

It was a female fox and it was, they had discovered, pregnant.

7

MARRIAGE AND THE FIRST
PUBLIC LECTURES

The second most common question I am asked about myself is: "Can you foretell your own future?"

(The *most* common is: "Can you use your gift to gamble, or play the stock market?" The answer to this is, unfortunately, no, I can't. I know because I've tried, but it simply doesn't work. Not for me, at any rate, although I have given business advice to clients and some of them, presumably, have used it in the stock market. I've never been paid any commission, though.)

Can I see my own future? The answer is yes and no, sometimes and occasionally. Whenever I *try* to find out what will happen in my own life, my gift turns out to be unreliable. I believe it is influenced by what I consciously or subconsciously *want* to happen. If I like the idea of something, or I'm looking forward to it, and I ask myself "Will it happen?" my gift always says yes, it will, and it will be just as you want it. But most of the time it doesn't happen. It's the same with my family, and sometimes with other people with whom I am very close. If I like them, I want things to happen for them, and somehow I am too involved with them to get a clear psychic impression of what is *actually* going to happen.

From time to time, however, I do get a real psychic impression of my own future. It doesn't happen when I look for it, but occasionally it comes out of the blue, as all my psychic impressions used to when I was young. I just *know*.

For example, on the evening of Boxing Day, 1951, I walked into a Breda café with a group of my friends. My spirits were at high tide; my practice was flourishing, especially in the light of my successful cases, and my self-confidence was at a peak.

A family group, father, son, and daughter, was dining at a table in the corner. I watched them for a long time, puzzled by an idea that seemed to be trying to struggle into my mind.

Then, suddenly, I knew. I got up, walked over to the table and addressed myself to the father. I said: "Hello, Dad."

The man looked up in surprise. "I beg your pardon?" he said.

"You shouldn't mind that I call you 'Dad,' " I told him. "In less than a year I will be married to your daughter. My name is Rien Dykshoorn. . . ."

Taken aback though he was, the father was equal to the situation. He smiled broadly and said: "Well, hello, Rien Dykshoorn. Sit down, *son*."

Then he turned to his daughter, his eyes twinkling. "Cora, say hello to this young man. He says he is going to marry you."

But if her father was amused, Cora Klooté was not. It was a cold eye she turned on me that night. She was sorry to disappoint me, she said, but I was very much mistaken.

I did not see her again for six months, but our second meeting started a courtship and we were married in October, 1952.

I was thirty-two, and marriage changed my life. Until then my gift had been the only constant in my life, and for a long time that had brought me more confusion and trouble than happiness. Cora brought a stability, a contentment, and a sense of both achievement and purpose that I had never known before. With her I was unassailable, and after our daughter, Helga, was born in 1955, my contentment was complete.

Curiously enough, while I had converted to Catholicism some years before, Cora had also become a Catholic before we met. Each of us had been born into Protestantism, and each of us, independently of the other, had converted to Catholicism.

I mention this because the priest I met in Breda while searching for the Host of Niervaart, Chaplain (and later Bishop) de Vet was not the only spiritual adviser of ours with whom I came into contact through my work. Another was Chaplain van Mechelen, whom we met shortly after our marriage. As it turned out, I was to do some work for him.

One night in our home I had a very strong psychic impression about his life.

"Listen," I said, "I see you being given a parish of your own very soon. Within six months, I think."

Chaplain van Mechelen replied with good humor that this was unlikely. There were no vacant parishes, he said, and all the incumbent pastors were in good health.

"I don't see it coming from anyone's death," I said. "I think it will be a new parish."

"But I don't have seniority," he insisted. "Even if a parish should become vacant, I would not be appointed."

"That's up to the bishop," I said. "And he will select you because you are the one for the job."

Then I worked it out further, and said that I saw him being welcomed to his new parish by a large crowd of people, some of them riding in horse-drawn carriages.

Chaplain van Mechelen chuckled. "Well, Rien, it is certainly a detailed prediction, even though I can't imagine that it will come true."

Some five months later he was appointed pastor in Breskens, a parish newly created by the bishop as part of a project to subdivide some of his larger parishes. And the first time he visited his new parish, Chaplain van Mechelen was met by a welcoming crowd—and to add to the charm of their welcome, some of them were riding in horse-drawn carriages.

He called on us a week or so later. He had dined with the bishop, he said, and told him that I had foretold the appointment even though the bishop himself had come to his decision only a matter of weeks before.

"I told the bishop: 'Dykshoorn knew about this months ago,' " he said. "And the bishop said: 'Ah, but that's Dykshoorn!' "

The bishop was Monseigneur Baeten, in whose favor Josef Opperman and I had relinquished our claims to the Host of Niervaart.

Marriage brought happiness, but it also brought additional responsibilities. Like most newlyweds, we were faced with a pressing need to secure our future. My practice was flourishing in Breda and I was gaining great satisfaction from it, but the financial rewards were small. At the same time, of course, I earned nothing from my work for the police.

The fact was, I had never been much concerned with the state of my finances. If I had enough with which to live, it was enough. Now, suddenly, I had to stabilize my affairs and decide in which direction I wanted to move in my work.

I needed to broaden my scope. My work on major cases had brought me a reasonable measure of fame in Holland and Belgium, but my practice in Breda remained essentially a provincial one.

It would be necessary for me to become more widely known, but at the same time I could not resort to sensational publicity-hunting, whatever the immediate rewards.

The obvious solution was for me to give public demonstrations of my abilities. If I could demonstrate my gift before large audiences, it would not take long for word to spread, and the natural result would be that more people would seek private consultations.

But I was reluctant to do it. I was reasonably sure that I could work before a large audience, but I had no desire to become known as an "entertainer," with a reputation similar to that of a stage magician or a comedian. I had no desire to enter show business.

Tricksters had been performing so-called acts of ESP on the

stage for years in mind-reading or telepathic performances, and several such acts had been publicly exposed as fraudulent, bringing the whole field of ESP into disrepute as far as public demonstrations were concerned.

Cora and I argued about it. She was convinced that a series of public lectures could not harm my professional image or lessen the esteem in which I was held by the authorities. I did not have to act or perform, she said, but simply work for people in public as I worked for them in private. By doing this, she said, I could show people the *real* possibilities of ESP, with all the usual gimmickry and trickery trimmed away.

Finally I agreed, but with one unalterable understanding—that I would never share a program with anyone else, psychic or not. My gift had to be judged on its merits alone, and the format would be a lecture–demonstration, never a show.

The first lecture was organized for the evening of November 19, 1952, at the Concordia Auditorium in Breda.

At my first sight of the audience, I quailed. I had no set plan to follow, and I was nervous as a kitten. What would the audience expect? More than I was able to give?

I decided that I would first try to explain my gift in simple terms, to make it clear what I could do and what I could not, and then invite the audience to ask me questions.

I told them I was not a telepathist; I could not tell anyone what he or she was thinking at a particular moment. Nor did I have the power to influence events, but only to see them as they had occurred or would occur in the future. I would answer any question provided it was asked in good faith and the questioner agreed to admit when I had given a correct answer on any point of known fact. If an answer seemed only slightly related to a question, there would be a reason for it. A more direct answer might embarrass the questioner, or I might not have been able to obtain a complete answer from my gift. In this case I would try to work it out as thoroughly as possible, but it might take time.

Then I invited the audience to ask me questions.

Was the lecture a success? I quote from the Breda daily news-paper *De Stem* of the following morning, November 20, 1952:

> . . . strong examples of clairvoyance made for an exciting and interesting evening. The audience at the Concordia wit-nessed several striking events.
>
> When a question had parapsychological interest, Mr. Dykshoorn went into it very deeply. A question regarding a family crest took him back to the seventeenth century, to the time the title was granted to the family concerned.
>
> The clairvoyant stated the year, 1680, very exactly, then told accurately the history of the crest ring. He also told why the title was lost in the last century, through a breaking of the line of heritage. Then Dykshoorn said that two en-gagement rings had been made from the crest ring, and this was correct.
>
> Regarding a presumed theft, Mr. Dykshoorn told who had committed the crime, a young girl psychologically unbal-anced by a kleptomania complex.
>
> From Dykshoorn's description the owner immediately rec-ognized the place where the stolen goods had been hidden.

In the wake of this unqualified success, Cora and I embarked on a busy program of lectures. Between November, 1952, and April, 1953, I gave more than twenty-five lecture–demonstrations, many of them in aid of charities.

Each time my basic presentation was the same. I would begin with a brief explanatory talk, stating what I was capable of doing with my psychic abilities, then I would invite the people to ask me questions.

This remains the basic format of my lectures today. I cannot explain what my gift is or how it works; I can only tell you what I can do, and then do it.

It is also far better if people ask questions to which they really want to know answers, or questions that will interest the rest of the audience, like the one above where the family wanted to know the history of their title and crest. The tendency at the beginning of the demonstration is for people to ask "How many children do I have?" or "What is my occupation?" These are "quiz" questions; they already know the answers. It is better if they ask questions about the past or the future, so that later, through their own research or the passing of time they can judge the value of a psychic gift.

Most audiences are surprised, too, that I don't merely answer one question, then go on to the next person. The purpose of the demonstration is to show how deeply my gift takes me into the lives of other people, so I will usually spend ten or fifteen minutes working with each questioner, telling as much as possible of what I see.

I have only one aim in the demonstrations—to show people how it really goes with ESP.

Our lecture tours took us to practically every corner of the Netherlands, and along the way we encountered some amusing incidents.

One Saturday found us in a small rural township where we had rented the local church hall for a lecture that evening. The response in neighboring towns had been excellent, so naturally we were expecting a full house.

But when the time came for the lecture, the hall was virtually empty. The public, as they say, stayed away in droves.

We were puzzled, and more than a little disappointed. But then, just as I was about to begin, the priest from whom we had rented the hall came hurrying out onto the stage.

"Mister Dykshoorn, I'm terribly sorry," he said. "I should have realized that you were depending on the local farmers to come along. But you see, they never go out on Saturday, because this is the night the whole family takes a bath!"

Not long after that we visited a small "twin town" on the border of Holland and Belgium. One half of the town was in Holland and the other half in Belgium, with the border running through the middle.

The attendance here was excellent and I went confidently into my lecture. But when I invited the audience to ask me questions, the hall was suddenly filled with an awkward, embarrassing silence. Not one hand was raised; no one wanted to ask a question.

Finally, after silence had reigned for long minutes on end, the mayor of the Dutch half of the town rose to thank me for my "speech."

"We all found the lecture most interesting, Mister Dykshoorn," he said. "And furthermore I suspect that tomorrow morning you will be kept more than busy with *private* consultations."

At his emphasis on the word "private," the audience suddenly erupted with laughter—much to my bewilderment—and there was a round of lusty cheering, hooting, and chiding of the mayor. I couldn't understand what the joke was supposed to be.

The following morning, however, it all came clear. I learned why none of my new clients—who were lined up by the dozens outside our hotel—had volunteered to question me in public the night before.

Almost without exception, the people who now came for *private* consultations were involved in petty smuggling from one side of town to the other (this was before the days of the Benelux agreement which opened the borders of Belgium, Holland, and Luxembourg). They had been wary of questioning me in public because I might have let something slip about their clandestine activities.

They may have been right, too, because a similar situation arose about a week later in another border town, and I could not resist informing them that I knew. A man stood up and asked "What is my occupation?" which is an old chestnut. I learned from my gift that he was a local tradesman, but I also saw that he dabbled in nocturnal border-crossings. So I said: "This is what I see, sir," and I got down on my hands and knees and started crawling across the stage.

Later the same evening a woman asked the other old standard: "How many children do I have?"

I said: "Well, Madam, last week you had only four. But yesterday you were walking in the street out in front like this"—I pushed my hands out in front of my stomach—"so I guess now you must have five!"

The woman, as her friends well knew, had indeed been "out in front" the day before, however, she had delivered not a fifth baby but a few dozen pairs of the best Belgian nylons!

Not all the incidents were amusing. In the town of Boxtel I was working before an animated audience of about four hundred and the questions were coming thick and fast. It was very hot and I was perspiring freely.

A man stood up and asked: "When will I be married?"

"Sir," I said, "you will be married within two years."

"Huh!" he snorted in disgust. "Listen, I am already well and truly married—with seven children! This is my wife sitting right beside me!"

The crowd immediately fell silent. I consulted my gift again and learned what would happen. Then I said: "Sir, you should have thought of that before you asked the question. I am sorry, but I can tell only what I see through my gift."

It took a while for the implication to take hold. If the man was to marry within two years, it would have to be after his present wife had been removed from the scene. The evening was ruined, the spontaneity replaced by a mood of tension and disquiet.

Two years later Cora and I returned to Boxtel, but the caretaker of the hall refused to rent to us. "People remember when you were here last," he said.

"What happened?" I asked.

"The man you said would marry within two years. His wife was killed in a motor accident only two months later. A lot of people believe it would never have happened if you hadn't said it."

"But I didn't say it," I protested. "Where is the man now?"

"He has remarried," the caretaker said.

This unfortunate episode caused me to change my attitude toward all questions asked from an audience. People insist on trying to trick me. I don't mind this in itself, but often they don't realize where their trick questions might lead. So from then on I adopted the practice of always using my gift to determine whether I am being asked a trick or loaded question, or a genuine one.

It takes a little longer, but it helps to avoid unpleasant incidents of this kind.

Most of my work for individual people, whether clients who came for consultations or people who asked questions from a lecture audience, involved looking into their personal lives. Parents wanted to know what would happen to their children. Men wondered about their careers or business. People were considering moving, or emigrating, or buying or selling. This was the standard line of questioning.

Occasionally, though, in those days, I found myself in the position of being able to offer more immediate help.

The magazine story from which the following passage is extracted appeared in *De Trom* ("The Drum"), July, 1953, issue. It followed a lecture I gave on behalf of the Young Men's Christian League in the town of Prinzenhague on June 21, 1953. The writer, a young man from the league, interviewed me after the lecture, and recounts an incident that took place.

> While we were sitting there quietly talking, someone telephoned from out of town and complained of severe headaches. Mr. Dykshoorn concentrated very deeply, then suddenly, from the telephone, we heard a shout of joy: "It's gone!"

I cannot explain this, except to say that it happened. The caller was a good friend of mine, and I decided to try and help him. I concentrated on him, felt him "come into me." I felt the pain of the headache, he lost it. What more can I say? I was as surprised as he was.

As it happened, at the lecture earlier the same evening I had helped a man in the same way. Concentrating on him, I felt his rheumatic pain and tried to take it out of him. It worked. *De Stem* reported on June 22, that *"the pain was pulled out of the man, so to speak."*

The most gratifying newspaper reports, however, were those that reported my demonstrations "straight," setting them apart from the mumbo jumbo that is often associated with ESP. On October 17, 1953, *De Stem* wrote:

> Dykshoorn is not a man who works with humbug. This we saw yesterday when he worked for the public in the Concordia auditorium.
>
> He did not give the impression of a man trying to force anything on the public or his audience. He works with complete honesty, without "fishing" or mysterious behavior.
>
> He worked so honestly that once he quietly conceded that he was unable to help because certain factors were not favorable.

During this period, one of the most deeply satisfying experiences of my life came when I delivered a lecture in the famous Pulchri Studio in The Hague. Almost five hundred people attended, filling the hall to its capacity, and many were from the diplomatic community, representing all parts of the world. But what gave me the most satisfaction was that this was the hall in which I had first heard Professor Greven speak, and first learned that I possessed a psychic gift. Now I was lecturing there, from the same dais, and the wheel had turned full circle.

8

YEARS OF RECOGNITION

The lectures brought me the measure of fame I needed to set my practice on a secure foundation. Clients came from all over the Low Countries and Germany and many came from as far afield as France and Denmark. The lecture tours took us to virtually every little corner of the Netherlands, and of course I continued to work as often as possible for the police.

Then early in 1954 a man came to see me with an unusual and challenging task for my gift. His name was Josef Oechsle, of Amsterdam, and he was the Netherlands' director of a West German organization called the *Volksbund Deutsche Kreigsgräber-fürforge*—the War–Graves Commission.

"It is my responsibility," he told me, "to locate the temporary graves in which German soldiers were buried in World War II, to identify the bodies, and arrange for proper burial of the remains. I understand that you have located human remains before, using your psychic abilities, and I wonder if you would be prepared to help me."

Herr Oechsle's job was a difficult one, for many reasons. This was not so long after the war that people had forgotten the unpleasantries of the occupation, and everywhere he went he met indifference and even hostility. Many people could not be bothered helping to find the bodies of German soldiers.

I not only accepted the work, but sought it eagerly. As long as parents, wives, and children could be relieved of the burden of uncertainty over the fate of their loved ones, and as long as my gift could bring the remains of human beings out of the bloody mud of history for decent burials, I had to volunteer my services freely. Death is apolitical, and makes no distinction between nationalities.

How to help, though, was another question. Without a name or an incident on which to center my concentration, I could hardly locate bodies buried across the length and breadth of the country.

Herr Oechsle solved this by supplying me with names and incidents, and I was able to help by "map-dowsing."

Two German soldiers, he told me, were believed to have drowned somewhere near Lanaeken and to have been buried as "unknown." Could I locate the unmarked graves?

I took my divining rod and worked over a map of the general area, waiting for the reaction of my gift that would tell me the area in which the bodies had been buried. It came—the point of the loop snapping down onto the paper. Then Herr Oechsle brought me a detailed ordnance map of the area and I worked over this in the same way. Again the loop snapped down to pinpoint a place.

Then I concentrated on the scene, and in my mind I saw the place. A cemetery, two unmarked graves. I calculated distances, described landmarks. Herr Oechsle took detailed notes, then went away to investigate in the field.

On July 20, 1954, he wrote to me as follows:

> It is my pleasure to inform you that I have succeeded in finding in Lommel the burial-places of the two German sol-

diers who in September 1944 were drowned in the Albertkanal near Lanaeken and were buried as unknown in the
cemetery for fallen German soldiers. This resulted directly
from instructions you gave me. (See Appendix.)

Josef Oechsle became a good friend and I worked for him whenever I could. Over the years we found many German soldiers by
map-dowsing. He would supply me with the name of a soldier or
recount to me an incident he had uncovered through his research,
and I would work over the maps with my divining rod.

Then in 1959 I worked on a special case which should be mentioned here. A German tank was known to have sunk in the River
Maas in 1944, but the place at which it sank had never been determined and the bodies of the crew had never been recovered.

Herr Oechsle brought me the maps and I worked it out. I quote
from the *VDK* journal *Kreigsgräber fürforge* of September 20,
1959:

. . . Herr Oechsle of Amsterdam traveled many hundreds
of kilometers to speak with sailors, mayors and local officials,
police and inhabitants of the area of the incident, but to no
avail.

Finally the well-known diviner Dykshoorn of Breda was
brought into the search. He volunteered his services for the
humanitarian cause without charge and expecting nothing
in return.

With the help of his divining rod he pointed out on a map
the exact location of the sunken tank, which he saw in the
Maas near a ferry, about five kms southwest of Roermund.

Now, after five years of searching, came the conclusion.
The tank was recovered. Three human destinies were resolved when the tank-soldiers were given a dignified burial.
One father was freed after fifteen years from the burden of
uncertainty over the fate of his son.

Without the efforts of those who search for years in the
service of the fallen and those who remain behind, *Feldwebel*
Ulrich Koneitzy would have been forever an unknown
soldier.

Feldwebel Ulrich Koneitzy had been the tank commander. I knew him. We had never met, but the moment I started searching for the tank, I knew him.

In August, 1955, the Dutch charitable organization the *Zonnebloem* ("Sunflower") asked me to undertake a series of public appearances in its aid. I agreed of course, and between September, 1955, and April, 1956, I gave more than sixty lectures to help this charity.

Our press clippings of the tour make a fat file, so I will quote from only a representative few, to give some idea of the kind of information my gift can supply to a person who asks me a question from the audience.

From *Het Nieuwsblad van het Zuiden,* Tilburg, September 22, 1955, comes this typical report:

> . . . It is a very exclusive method Mr. Dykshoorn uses. He does not require photographs or objects as inductors. One calls out a question and with only his divining rod, a simple piece of wire, Dykshoorn concentrates on the person concerned.
>
> He impersonates that person in gestures, posture, and peculiarities with startling exactness, and he is able to tell countless details from the past, the present, and also the future.
>
> Last night many questions were put to him by the audience. A father asked about the future possibilities of his son, and had to accept Mr. Dykshoorn's reply that "the boy had a genuine talent in the field he had already chosen, and in time would reach his set goal."
>
> An intending emigrant was told that he would succeed overseas but would not stay long in the first country of his choice. He would move on to another country he already had in mind.
>
> A lady was told that her son who had emigrated would soon return home.
>
> These are only a handful of the questions put to Mr. Dykshoorn. To one questioner he described in every tiny detail an office mentioned in the question, even down to a

description of an ashtray on the desk. The questioner could only acknowledge the description.

Mr. Dykshoorn earns special mention for the fact that in describing people and circumstances he always remains considerate. But in spite of the fact that he works without showmanship, his sympathetic manner captivated the audience for hours.

The next report covers one of those evenings in which, as I mentioned before, I was able to help a man by relieving him of some of his rheumatic pain. The report comes from the *Provinciale Noord-Brabantse Courant* of September 29, 1955:

CLAIRVOYANT AMAZES CROWD IN UDEN
AN ORDINARY MAN DOES EXTRAORDINARY THINGS

Martin van Hees from Volkel found himself in the crowd who came to watch, question, and listen to the clairvoyant Dykshoorn in the Heymericks Hall on behalf of the Zonnebloem.

Martin van Hees was told by Dykshoorn that he had a pain, a terrible pain, and that it was located in the hip.

The hall was very silent as Dykshoorn rubbed himself on the same part of the body, then asked if Mr. van Hees was still in pain.

Martin van Hees stood up, shook his head a little, then declared openly that the pain had disappeared!

Many remarkable things happened during the evening. Mr. Dykshoorn worked for a worthy cause, the welfare of the sick.

His achievements were unique.

In Dutch cattle markets, trading is carried out under a long-standing system of trust and agreement. When a buyer and seller have agreed on a price for a beast, the deal is settled with a traditional handshake and no more is said about money until all the traders—known as *veehandelaren*—gather at the end of the day in a bar or coffee house to settle up.

The traders take a fierce pride in their collective honesty. A *veehandelar*'s handshake is his bond. Although nothing is written down at the time of the agreement, no deal is ever forgotten and no price can be changed after the handshake. They never even ask one another for names or addresses.

In March of 1956 my gift led me to clear up a case that had shaken this traditional system to its foundations.

I was lecturing for the *Zonnebloem* in the Midden Brabant town of St. Oedenrode when a *veehandelar* named van der Leeuwen stood up to ask my advice on a particular problem.

"Last December I was at the market in s'Hertogenbosch," he said. "I settled a deal with another *veehandelar* with a handshake, and he took my cow away for shipment. He never turned up at the café, and I am out 837 guilders!"

I was surprised. A *veehandelar* had failed to honor a deal? The cow had been shipped off to an unknown destination, the buyer had never paid. One *veehandelar* had cheated another, or so it seemed.

I concentrated my gift on the problem, and worked it out. "Sir," I said, "your animal is in De Purmer, just north of Amsterdam. The buyer is a butcher in that district. He did not intend to cheat you, but he took ill that day and had to hurry away. Since he does not know who you are, he has not been able to send you the money. He has been ill for some time and his two sons are running the business. I am convinced you will find the man and get your money."

A couple of days later, van der Leeuwen contacted a shipping agent who regularly transported cattle from the market in s'Hertogenbosch to the Amsterdam area. If I was right and the buyer did live near Amsterdam and was a butcher in De Purmer, then perhaps the agent's records might offer a clue.

They did. The freight charge on a cow shipped from s'Hertogenbosch on December 28 had not been paid. The destination: De Purmer.

At the address listed, van der Leeuwen found the butcher D.V.*
He was the father of two sons who had taken over his business
while he continued to buy for them. He had left the market in
s'Hertogenbosch because of a sudden illness. He was still bed-
ridden.

He paid up the 837 guilders (about $250), out of which van
der Leeuwen sent me a fee. Accompanying it was the message:
"A *veehandelar* always keeps his word."

All this time I was working on police cases, and although for
most of them I was never able to gather any documentation, one
case should be mentioned here.

In the late fifties in West Germany, police investigating a ghastly
series of mutilation murders had detained a suspect they were
certain was responsible. All the circumstantial evidence pointed to
this man as the killer, but the police psychiatrists could not determine *why* this man had been driven to acts of such unspeakable
savagery. Desperately—and quite sincerely—he denied any knowledge of the murders, and to all appearances he was a stable, well-
behaved citizen.

He was clearly an advanced psychotic, a schizophrenic who
"flipped" into a murderously psychopathic state in which he committed his brutal acts—but what caused him to "flip"? He could
not be detained indefinitely on the basis of the evidence in hand.
Accordingly, unless the psychiatrists could prove he was dangerously psychotic—unless they could induce his schizoid change of
personality—he would have to be released.

I worked with the police criminologists and psychiatrists, never
meeting the suspect but only observing him in his prison cell in
Dusseldorf. Even so I worked him out. He had been unbalanced

---

* The man's name was not mentioned in the newspaper report of the case,
which was in the weekly *Midden Brabant*, March 30, 1956. He was referred to as "D.V." throughout, possibly because of the scandal the case
caused among the *veehandelaren*.

by a severely traumatic experience in his childhood, and whenever he was confronted with circumstances that reminded him of this awful experience, he would revert to his psychopathic state.

In his normal, placid state he could never recall the childhood trauma, but the moment he encountered a situation that brought the unbearable memory back, he blacked out in his mind while the uncontrollable instincts of his mind wreaked terrible revenge on the people who had "wronged" him. Afterward he was unable to remember anything that occurred during these blacked-out periods.

Through my gift I was able to describe the exact circumstances that would cause him to "flip." And when police officers staged a similar scene in his presence, he became violently enraged and tried to attack the officers.

The poor man, genuinely unaware of what he had done, was later declared legally insane.

Lectures and police cases, for all that they were enjoyable on the one hand and important on the other, took up only a small portion of my working time. For the most part, I worked for clients, in consultation, giving advice on personal and business problems.

Not all my clients, however, were individuals. Very often I worked for companies, working out business and even technical problems.

One Dutch firm of shoe manufacturers used my services on a regular basis for many years. Marketing executives would bring each season's new designs to me for advice on which would be the most successful, and I would go over each design, in turn, nominating those that precipitated favorable reactions from my gift.

In this procedure I relied entirely on my psychic impressions. I had no specialized knowledge of the footwear industry, apart from what I picked up over the years working for this company. However, by virtue of my psychic gift, I was able to know "instinctively" which designs would sell and which would not. My advice was always noted and followed. In any event, the executives kept coming back, year after year.

Once I was asked by the owner of a Breda construction company to assist in a matter of tenders submitted for a bank complex in Tilburg. The company had been one of six competing for the contract, but another Breda company had underbid them by a considerable amount—120,000 guilders, in fact.

"My problem," the builder told me, "is that I badly need this contract because it should lead to others in the future. But I can't trim my quote any further and still make a profit; if I go down to the other company's figure I will lose money on the job. Nevertheless, I am prepared to take the risk if you feel other contracts will result from this one."

I worked it out. "Stick to the figure you have quoted," I told him. "It is a fair price and you will get the job anyway. The other company has made a clerical error in its estimate and will withdraw."

About a month later the builder called to say the opposition company had withdrawn and he had been awarded the contract.

On another occasion I was retained by a large Dutch shipbuilding concern to assist with a more serious problem. One of their ships had suffered severe warpage of the curved steel plates cladding the funnel. The fault was obviously a metallurgical one, but the management was worried that testing of many plates at different locations would lead to production stoppages and much unnecessary expense, especially since most of the plates would prove to be sound.

They wondered if I could locate the faulty plates among the thousands of others.

It was a complicated problem, and I knew the company had brought me in only on the off-chance that I might save them a great deal of time, trouble, and money. For hours I pored over the blueprints of ships and factories and warehouses and riveting sites and even lists of storage bays, relying entirely on the reactions of my gift while the executives took detailed notes.

Finally we came up with a list of locations at which I believed they would find faulty plates. Then I decided to try and take it one step further. The plates had obviously been rolled from a faulty ingot, and through a coding system each plate had chalked on it the ingot batch from which it had been rolled and the date it had left the rolling mill.

I took an ordinary calendar and asked the executives to call off the days, going backward in time. When the reaction came, I told them the date on which the faulty ingot had been rolled.

Some time later I received a report from the company. They had found faulty plates at each of the locations I had listed, and at no others. The chalked code also showed that the faulty plates had been rolled on exactly the day my gift had indicated.

Then in 1958 I worked on a purely technical problem for a machine-tool company in the Ruhr region of West Germany.

This company's engineers were trying to perfect the design of an automatic packing machine. It seemed that other machines bound packages and crates with half-inch metal strips, but these metal bands cut from sheet were sharp-edged and tended to damage packages under the stresses of transportation. The new machine would bind backages with bands of a strong but more resilient nylon-and-plastic material.

The problem was that the resilience that gave the material its advantage over metal also made it impossible to clip the ends together tightly enough to ensure against slippage under stress. The nylon-and-plastic material was subject to what was called "molecular memory." No matter how tightly the ends were clipped or tied, the material would always revert, however slightly, to its original flat shape.

I worked over the blueprints trying to pinpoint the area of the problem, and finally my gift brought into my mind a clear impression of how the finished machine would look after the problem was resolved. Two little power-driven grinding wheels would be installed to grind the ends before they were clipped.

Then I drew a rough diagram of the grinding wheels and showed the engineers where I saw the wheels being installed in the machine itself.

Like all aspects of my work, this is difficult to explain in logical terms, but I solved this problem not by trying to find a solution of my own, not by asking myself "how *can* it be solved?" but instead by asking myself "how *will* it be solved?" The answer of the two little grinding-wheels was not really my own answer to the technical problem, even though it was on my suggestion that they were installed. I "saw" that this would happen, that the final, finished machine would have these wheels installed, while the prototype did not.

If I had not been involved, perhaps the engineers would have found this solution themselves. To some extent, it's an academic question. Somehow I was able to act as intermediary in this case, bridging the gap between the present problem and the solution that would be found in the future, which enabled the engineers to work out the technicalities of how the wheels would be installed.

9

"TELEFONVISION"—LONG-DISTANCE CLAIRVOYANCE

Most of my work is done in private consultation with individual clients, and these consultations generally follow the form I have outlined earlier. The client asks me a direct question about something he or she wants to know, and I concentrate my gift on the particular question and the people involved with it. The client sits in front of me and answers yes or no to questions of known fact, so that I can tell whether or not I am on the right track.

Often it takes some time to arrive at the answer to the client's specific question, and this is why I prefer to work face-to-face with my client.

On occasion, though, I have been able to work over the telephone. I never know for sure if I am going to be able to do it, but occasionally I have tried, and occasionally it has worked.

In 1958 I worked on two cases in quick succession over telephone lines—long-distance telephone lines, from my home in Breda, Holland, to Ruhrort, near Duisburg in West Germany, 240 miles away.

There was an interesting prelude to the case. While I was well known in Holland and Belgium as a result of my lecturing and the publicity that had followed such cases as the search for the Host of Niervaart and those in which I had found bodies, I was not so well known to the public in West Germany. I had done a lot of work there for individual clients and companies and also for the police, but none of these cases had reached the ears of the press. My work for clients was, of course, confidential, and in line with my standing arrangement with all the European police forces for whom I worked, my activity on murder cases was always performed in the strictest secrecy.

As far as lectures went, I could not lecture in Germany simply because I possessed only a very halting command of the language. Cora was fluent in German, but we had found that without a good command of the language, I could not maintain the continuity of question-and-answer necessary for an effective public demonstration of my gift.

Then toward the end of 1957 I was asked by the police in Dusseldorf to assist in a murder case, and while I was there a young reporter from *Der Mittag* tracked me down at my hotel. He knew why I was in town and, confronting me on the hotel steps, he fired off a lot of questions about the murder case.

Because of my arrangement with the police, I couldn't answer any of his questions, so I kept answering "no comment." Then he started speculating, and reported rumors he had heard of my activities in connection with the case.

Finally I said to him in German: *"Ich mache keinen Hokuspokus."* Meaning: "I don't make hocus-pocus."

Eventually he went away and wrote his story in which he speculated on the extent of my involvement with the murder investigation, and to headline his story he used my exact words: *"Ich mache keinen Hokuspokus!"*

It wasn't important, but it was timely, because only a few months later I was all over the German newspapers, for having solved two cases by *"telefonvision."*

It was late in the evening of March 25, 1958, when I received my first long-distance telephone call from Franz-Josef Becker. He was the owner and captain of a Rhine barge, one of those utilitarian craft that ply tirelessly up and down the great river from Rotterdam to Lake Constance with the cargoes that keep Europe functioning. He was calling from Ruhrort, near Duisburg in West Germany, 240 miles away from Breda, and he had a problem.

"My boat has been stolen," he said. "Not my barge, but my tender, my launch. It has been missing for two days. I have looked everywhere around here and asked people if they've seen it, but without any results. It cost two-and-a-half thousand marks, my launch, but it means more than that to me. Without it I can't do business, and you have to wait months for delivery for a new one."

"Well, sir," I said, "What do you want me to do about it?"

"I don't know," he said. "I've been to the river police in Duisburg, but they haven't been able to find it. Then my wife suggested you might be able to help. She is Dutch, you see. . . ."

At first, I didn't think I could help the man, but since he had gone to the trouble of calling me long distance, I decided to try. I took up the divining rod and concentrated on the problem.

And I worked it out. "Your boat hasn't been stolen," I said. "Some teenagers set it adrift. You will find it about two-and-a-half kilometers downstream, under a bridge. It is caught in the shallows, but it is undamaged."

I had seldom been more certain of a psychic impression. In Ruhrort, Becker went to the river police and told them what I had said, and they went with him to check it out. Two-and-a-half kilometers downstream, under a bridge, in the shallows, its mooring-rope drifting free, was the launch.

Becker phoned me again. "I am going to send you a check," he said.

But our dealings were far from over. The launch was found on the morning of March 26. Two days later, on March 28, in the evening, Franz-Josef Becker phoned me again, long distance from Ruhrort.

"You won't believe this," he said, "but tonight my wife and I

went to a café in the town, and when we got back to our barge
we found that my cabin had been broken into and my money
stolen. I lost 280 German marks and 150 Dutch guilders. Can you
help again?"

"This is a criminal case," I said. "You have notified the police,
haven't you?"

"Yes, of course," he said.

"In fact," I said, "they are listening on another line, aren't
they?"

Becker laughed. "You are right again," he said. "But listen, can
you tell me who stole my money?"

I worked it out, while Becker and the police waited on the line.
"I see five barges moored alongside one another. Which one is
yours?"

"The one farthest from the bank," he said.

"All right. Now, there is a big one at the other end of the line,
nearest the bank. It is a fifteen-hundred tonner. It has a crew of
three and one of them is a young man about seventeen. He is
leaving in the morning for his vacation. He is the one who stole
your money and it is in his travel bag."

Then we rang off and I heard no more about it until the following evening. Cora and I were listening to the radio when the
news came over the air: "Clairvoyant Dykshoorn solves a robbery
case by telephone, long distance from Holland to Germany."

Becker and the Duisburg river police went to the fifteen-
hundred-ton barge moored nearest to the shore at the same wharf
as Becker's. The captain had a crew of three. The police asked the
captain if one of them was planning to leave the next day for his
vacation.

The captain said: "How do you know that? He only spoke to
me about it ten minutes ago!"

The crewman was a young boy of seventeen. The police searched
his cabin and found in his travel bag two envelopes containing
280 marks and 150 guilders. He had not even had time to take
the money out of Becker's own special envelopes.

Becker went immediately to the press, radio, and television with his story of how I had solved the case by telephone—which was why I myself first heard about it on the radio. Then the reporters checked with the police for confirmation of the story and the police told them: "Yes, Dykshoorn solved the case by telephone —long distance!"

The story was picked up by DPA, the West German cable service, and ran all over Europe from Denmark to Italy. And in their characteristic fashion, the journalists coined a word to describe what I had done. I had solved the case, they said, by *telefonvision.*

Eventually, as a result of all the publicity, I was invited by the press of the Ruhr region to hold a press conference and demonstrate my psychic abilities in Duisburg as soon as possible. They wanted to examine my abilities for themselves.

Cora and I went down on May 12. I was very nervous, and not only because I would have to demonstrate my abilities in Dutch while Cora acted as interpreter. Unlike the lectures I had given in Holland and Belgium, this would not be a straightforward demonstration to an essentially sympathetic audience of people who had come because they were interested in ESP and my work.

The *"telefonvision"* case had caused a sensation in Germany, and this conference would be attended by about thirty journalists from newspapers, magazines, radio stations, and television channels. I knew I could expect to be challenged by some of the keenest, most analytical, and possibly most cynical minds in Europe.

The press conference was held in the Schloms Restaurant in Ruhrort. Was it a success? I leave it to the reader to judge from some of the resulting stories:

From *Der Mittag*, Dusseldorf, May 13, 1958:

> "The devil will have it! The rheumatism is gone!"
> An important shipbroker, weighing 200 pounds, shouted this sentence in Ruhrort yesterday when the Dutch psychic

Marinus Bernardus Dykshoorn took away his rheumatism in a few seconds.

For more than three years the broker had been tortured by this pain. Now he could do knee-bends. It was amazing—astounding!

Apart from the healing of the broker's rheumatism, Dykshoorn told a young man that he had failed once in school. This was correct.

To a couple who had come from the Eastern Zone he described the position, magnitude, and surroundings of a textile business they had owned.

In reply to the question from one guest: "Which radical changes in my life have taken place in the last few weeks?" Dykshoorn left us dumbfounded.

"Yes," he said, "you were divorced last week."

This last questioner was a personal friend of this reporter, and I guarantee that Dykshoorn did not know the people concerned.

And from *Abendpost,* Frankfurt, May 13, 1958:

> . . . There are 30 people in the clubroom, three of whom I know very well, and I know that they have never seen or heard from Dykshoorn and that he had no opportunity to talk to them beforehand.
>
> We are all excited.
>
> "Please ask me questions," says the Dutchman.
>
> One of my friends asks: "How will my business further develop?" He is a shipbroker.
>
> Dykshoorn concentrates, then suddenly he stares at the shipbroker and says: "Barge-owners will sell their boats to you. You are a shipbroker, are you not?"
>
> We are speechless.

Curiously enough, the *Abendpost* story mentions that I was able to identify one man as a shipbroker, and that he was a personal friend of the reporter, while *Der Mittag* reports that I was able to relieve a shipbroker of his rheumatic pain. In fact, it was the same man. The moment I turned my concentration on him, I knew that he was suffering from this pain and, as had happened before in other cases, I was able to provide him with some relief.

The Becker cases were not the only ones in which I was able to use my *"telefonvision,"* although they were the most publicized. Late in 1960, only a matter of days before we left Europe for Australia, I had a telephone call from a Mr. Spensoux in Charleroi, Belgium. His valuable pedigreed dog had disappeared, and he wondered whether I could help.

"I see the dog tied up in the yard of a building," I told him. "I don't know, but I think it is a factory of some kind. Perhaps it is a bakery; I smell fresh bread. And I think the building is pink and white—half pink and half white, as though it is being painted. Do you know a place like that in Charleroi?"

"I think I do," he said.

We were due to leave Breda the following day to catch our plane from The Hague to Australia. In the morning Mr. Spensoux tried to phone, but we had already had our telephone disconnected. So he sent us a telegram, stating that the dog had been found by the security guard of a Charleroi bakery. It was tied on a leash in the yard. The bakery, which had been white, was in the process of being painted pink.

10

THE SEARCH FOR
CAPTAIN GUYNEMER

Captain Georges Guynemer is a legendary figure in French history. He was the French "Ace of Aces" in World War One—the French Rickenbacker or von Richtofen. A winner of the Legion d'Honneur, Guynemer was leader of the famous Escadrille des Cignones —the "Stork Squadron"—and he personally shot down more than fifty German aircraft in duels over the western front. Guynemer was the dominant French hero in an age of heroes—the personification of courage, gallantry, and patriotism.

But on September 11, 1917, Guynemer paid for his daring. During the savage battle for Flanders his light plane was shot down by German ground fire, plunging to earth in the midst of heavy fighting around Poelcapelle, not far from Ypres in Belgium.

Not much is known about his end. His plane crashed behind German lines and his body was buried by the German infantry, but the exact location of the grave was not recorded and his remains have never been recovered.

A place of honor is reserved for Guynemer in the Panthéon in Paris; if his remains are ever found he will lie in state with the great French heroes of the ages.

The first official search for his grave was mounted immediately after the armistice of 1918. But the flat fields of Poelcapelle had been devastated beyond recognition, and no trace of Guynemer was found. His remains could have been almost anywhere beneath the shell-torn, blood-soaked earth.

Since 1918 many attempts have been made to pinpoint Guynemer's last resting place, but none has met with success.

In 1959 I conducted my own search for Guynemer. The case was one of the most important of my life. From a parapsychological viewpoint, I believe it is the only case of its kind ever to be recorded.

I instituted the search myself. Until 1959 I had never heard of Georges Guynemer or the mystery of his missing remains. I read about them in the Dutch weekly magazine *Panorama*, which told of an unsuccessful attempt to locate the grave by a French military research group headed by a Colonel de Sainte-Pereuse.

This commission, convened amid some controversy following provocative remarks in another magazine article, examined historical documents and heard testimony, some of it contradictory, from survivors of the Battle of Flanders. An old infantry veteran named Hemerlynck testified that he had seen Guynemer's grave at the time of the last Flanders offensive, and two brothers named Vercaigne claimed to have seen after the armistice a corpse clad in a leather flying-jacket which might have been the hero's distinctive Escadrille des Cignones jacket.

The commission's research had come to nothing, but the article in *Panorama* had a profound effect on me. The case struck me as the most interesting and challenging I had ever encountered, and my psychic impressions about it were enormously strong. I knew that Guynemer was still there under the ground, where he had been buried in 1917, and even now, after forty years, I was convinced I could find him.

I told Cora: "We're going to Ypres to search for this man. I believe I can find him."

Cora was against the idea at first. I had a lot of commitments in Breda, and she was worried that I might overextend myself. She thought I should wait until I felt less tired and had fewer cases waiting for my attention.

But my enthusiasm was aroused. I wrote to the mayor of the municipality of Poelcapelle asking for permission to search for Guynemer in the district. I said that I would absorb all my own expenses and that if I found Guynemer's remains I would donate them freely to the French government. I would need the mayor's assistance to move with some freedom in the district because I might possibly have to venture onto private property.

The mayor replied cautiously, and on March 12 Cora and I went down to Ypres. We met with the mayor, two aldermen, and the government-appointed council secretary. Arrangements were settled for a search in April, with the council smoothing the way and providing digging facilities if needed. I asked for and was given detailed maps of the area in which Guynemer's plane was believed to have gone down, then Cora and I drove the 250 miles back to Breda.

But the fact that I was confined to Breda did not prevent me from working on the case. By map-dowsing, working with the divining rod over the maps spread across my desk, I established that Guynemer's plane had, in fact, gone down at the place generally accepted as the site of the crash.

The psychic impressions entered my mind with a force and clarity that surprised me even though I had been experiencing them all my life. In my mind I saw what Guynemer had seen in the last seconds of his last flight: trenches, fighting, trees stripped and ravaged, farm buildings shattered by artillery fire but still standing . . . and I saw Guynemer's light biplane plummet to earth in the midst of it all. It broke up, but it did not explode or catch fire.

"The Germans would not have transported the body too far

from the wreckage," I reasoned to Cora. "It was trench warfare—they would have buried him as quickly as possible."

Then, still by map-dowsing, I worked out on a survey map the exact spot at which the plane had crashed in relation to the buildings standing on that particular field. All I had to do, I thought, was start from that point and "divine" for the body as I had searched for the old man in the canal in Sluis.

We went down on April 15, a cold, wet, miserable spring day in Belgium. Another conference was held in the mayor's chambers and the secretary agreed to accompany us on the search. Then we set out in our car for the field my divining rod had picked out on the map.

Had Guynemer been with us he might not have recognized the flat, fertile fields as those over which he had seen such battles raging. Crops had been cultivated over the terrain where men had given their lives for mere yards of ground. But on this gray, drizzling day it was easy to imagine the hardship and misery the soldiers of both sides must have endured.

Then as we approached the field and came in sight of the farm buildings, I had a strange feeling that something was wrong.

"Stop the car," I said, and got out.

We were about a quarter of a mile short of the buildings, yet I felt that we had come far enough. The buildings looked unfamiliar. I wanted to go onto the field, but a deep ditch ran alongside the road and the only access was by way of a bridge farther down the road, closer to the buildings.

We walked down and crossed the bridge to stand on the edge of the rainswept field. This was the field on which Guynemer had died—I was certain of it—but still I felt that something was wrong.

"In 1917," I said, "these buildings were not here. There were other buildings, but they have gone and these have been built since. The original buildings were back down the road, closer to where we stopped the car."

The secretary said he did not know of other buildings having stood on that field, but he acknowledged that this was the place eyewitnesses agreed had been the site of Guynemer's crash. "Red Cross observers noted this area," he said.

At that moment we were approached by a man who introduced himself as Rene Oosterlynck, farmer and owner of the property.

The secretary explained why we were there and asked if we could dig in his field if we considered it necessary. He said that was all right as long as his farming was not disrupted nor his pasture seriously damaged.

Then I asked him: "Were your buildings standing in 1917? I have an idea there were other buildings back down the road."

"No," he said. "The old buildings were pulled down after the war, but these were built on the same foundations. There have never been other buildings on this property. You can take my word for it."

I didn't want to take his word for it, so I asked the secretary to check the municipal records. Those buildings did not look right to me.

We went back to Ypres, spent a pleasant night at the Sultan Hotel, then met the secretary again the following morning.

"I checked the records," he said. "There were never any other buildings on the field."

It was another cold, miserable, drizzling day. I still didn't feel happy about it, but this was the right field and here, it seemed, were the buildings. I paced off my distances and went to work with the divining rod, searching for a body under the ground.

For this I used a very simple method. The reason most of the cases in which I found bodies were so straightforward and so quickly completed is that I simply hold the divining rod in my hands and move about waiting for a reaction, just as a water-diviner waits until his reaction tells him he is over water. I don't actually see anything in my mind while doing this; it's purely a matter of getting a reaction from the divining rod. While concentrating on Guynemer himself during his last living moments I had received clairvoyant, clairaudient, and clairsensory impressions, but those had stopped at the moment of his death and the crash of his plane. Now I was simply "dowsing" for human remains.

For about ten minutes I tramped about in the mud with the wire in my hands. Suddenly the point of the wire loop flicked down!

"Dig here!" I said.

We dug—and less than two feet deep in the soil we unearthed several bones and some teeth!

Guynemer? The secretary let out a cry of astonishment. "Stop digging!" he cried. "Stop digging! I must notify the authorities! The mayor! The French consul! The government! If this is Guynemer. . . ."

We stopped digging. He hurried back to Ypres. The mayor telephoned the French consul-general in the nearby town of Ghent, one Monsieur Jamme, who in turn contacted Paris. M. Jamme said he would personally come to Ypres as soon as possible.

Cora and I went back to the Sultan to wait. This was Thursday, and over the weekend an official party gathered in Ypres. It consisted finally of M. Jamme, another French diplomat, M. Jacques Haxo, from the Ministère des Anciens Combattants et Victimes de Guerre in Paris, and a specialist in exhumation, Dr. Gunther P. Schulz, with an assistant. Dr. Schulz and his assistant had driven six hundred miles from Göttingen, in West Germany, without rest.

A meeting was held Monday morning in the mayor's chambers. Dr. Schulz and his assistant had exhumed the remains and were to announce their findings. That meeting remains crystal-clear in my memory to this day.

The tension was heavy as Dr. Schulz entered carrying the remains in a metal box, and his eyes caught and held mine as he made his announcement.

"Mister Dykshoorn," he said, very slowly and dispassionately. "I have examined these remains very thoroughly, and have finalized my conclusions. There is no doubt in my mind that these are the remains of . . . a pig."

A pig! What a moment! For the first time in my life I wished my gift could make me disappear! I had gone out to divine for human remains, never dreaming that my gift would react to animal bones as well as human! Instead of Guynemer, I had unearthed the remains of some long-buried and long-since-forgotten barnyard pig!

M. Jamme went back to Ghent. The others stayed in Ypres to rest and recover from the anticlimax. It was decided that as long as the experts remained on hand, workmen would continue digging, enlarging the hole in case human remains lay deeper in the soil or close nearby.

Cora and I went out to watch. I was deeply puzzled. In Breda I had felt strongly that a search for Guynemer would prove fruitful, but now I felt equally strongly that he was nowhere close by. Something was wrong—with the terrain, the field, the buildings. Especially the buildings.

More animal bones were unearthed during the morning, then the workmen broke off for lunch.

Suddenly Cora became very excited. "The buildings!" she exclaimed. "There *must* have been others. You felt it. The records, the secretary, the farmer, they must all be wrong. And if there *were* other buildings, there might be foundations—farther down, where we first stopped the car. You might find them by divining! Then if there were other buildings . . ."

We walked down the field three or four hundred yards and I started divining, looking for old foundations. Within minutes the reaction came. We ran back and borrowed two of the workmen's spades, then we dug.

By the time the workmen came back from their lunch break,

we had uncovered an old fireplace and part of the foundations of a wall. The Oosterlynck buildings had *not* been built on the foundations of the old, original buildings!

Then I began divining again for human remains, and when the reaction came this time, I knew there were human remains beneath my feet. Cora and I dug, and again we uncovered a bone. But this time it did not look like the bone of an animal.

Cora took the bone, wrapped it in cloth and drove quickly back to Ypres. M. Haxo, Dr. Schulz, and his assistant were lunching at the Sultan. Cora rushed in, took the bone from the cloth and handed it to Dr. Schulz right across his plate.

"We found this in the field," she said. "At another place, farther down—and there *are* old foundations!"

Dr. Schulz never lost his composure for an instant. He took the bone, examined it and then, as mildly as he had made his previous announcement, identified it as the femur, or thigh bone, of a human male!

By the time Cora, the two doctors, and M. Haxo arrived back at the farm—having contacted M. Jamme again and notified him of the new find—the workmen and I had unearthed several more bones, all of them from human beings. Dr. Schulz and his assistant took over the exhumation, gently lifting the bones from the mud, tagging them and storing them in aluminum cases.

This was Monday. By Tuesday evening we had found six complete human skeletons. All had been men in their late teens, and all had lain in the earth since the time of the battle for Flanders. In addition to the bodies, we found German army registration plates, several bayonets, pieces of World War One weapons and communications equipment, buttons from English and German uniforms, and a wallet containing legible papers including a letter written in 1917, but never sent, to a Friedrich Schuster in Dusseldorf. All the bodies and materials lay in a buried trench which had not been known to exist by military historians; it had not been shown on any map or chart of the battlefield.

The authorities, needless to say, were astounded. M. Haxo's

French government ministry had suddenly been presented with the remains of six human beings killed in a war more than forty years earlier, along with dozens of relics, and I had located all of them by purely psychic means.

None of the skeletons, however, was that of Guynemer. Using the hero's dental charts from his service record and comparing them with the teeth of the skeletons we had found, Dr. Schulz and his assistant examined every possibility that one of them was Guynemer, but none was.

Then on Wednesday morning I found another skeleton, the seventh, but this was not Guynemer's, either. And now the case started getting complicated.

One factor was the weather. It rained without respite, and by Wednesday afternoon the excavations had bogged down to the point where it was almost physically impossible to dig any further in the liquid mud.

Furthermore, all the officials and diplomats involved had duties waiting elsewhere. With no certainty that Guynemer would be found, and no certainty that his remains would be identifiable, it was obvious the search could not go on indefinitely.

When news of the discoveries reached the press, reporters from all over France, Belgium, Holland, and Germany converged on Ypres, adding their own particular brand of confusion to the scene, dogging our footsteps everywhere.

These were the external complications, but I was experiencing some internal confusion as well. For one thing, I was not certain that Guynemer's remains could be found without a lot more digging. I had found seven bodies in Oosterlynck's farm, but not the specific one I was looking for. There were still some aspects of the case that would not come clear in my mind, even though the question of the buildings had been resolved.

I had very clear psychic impressions of Guynemer himself— I could "see" him in my mind—but, strangely enough, he seemed to "walk away" from me. It was as though he was trying to lead me away from the area in which I was sure his remains were buried. Why? Some information was being withheld from me, but I couldn't put my finger on what it was. Was it that I couldn't understand my own psychic impressions, or was it something else?

Then, to compound my problems, a rumor started around Ypres that M. Haxo's department had agreed to pay me one thousand francs for each World War One corpse recovered. Of course, this was not true; far from profiting from the case, I was bearing all my own expenses—and we had already been in Poelcapelle a full week.

I held a press conference to set the record straight. I was not being paid either for my work or for the bodies and relics I had found. I had not found Captain Guynemer, nor was I certain I could do so, although I believed he was buried somewhere nearby.

Then I told the reporters something I had learned through my gift. The search would be called off the next day, I said, when the farmer Rene Oosterlynck presented a claim for damages. He had not done so at the time, but I knew he would do so.

I was right. The next morning Rene Oosterlynck informed M. Haxo that he considered his pasture had been excessively damaged by the digging and that, regretfully, he felt obliged to seek compensation.

His claim was justified, of course. After all the digging his farm had begun to resemble the battlefield it had once been, and the sudden invasion of reporters, workmen, officials, and onlookers had completely disrupted the operation of his business, which was, after all, farming.

A meeting was held in the town hall. I agreed to pay five hundred francs to the farmer if the French government would pay the remaining one thousand francs of the claim. M. Jamme agreed and the meeting broke up.

Upon emerging from the town hall, the officials were amazed to find news of the claim in the morning newspapers—which had been printed before Oosterlynck had even presented it.

So the die was cast. Guynemer had to be found without any

further digging, and since this was clearly impossible, the search was over.

Cora and I went back to Breda without having found Guynemer. But the case had still been one of the most successful of my life. The facts were indisputable and the witnesses unimpeachable. I had found seven human bodies by psychic divining.

Why was I unable to find Guynemer? Why did my gift lead me to the bodies of seven other soldiers in Oosterlynck's field, but not to Guynemer's?

I believe in destiny. I believe that there are patterns in life and they will fall into place eventually, one way or another. In Breda at the beginning I felt very strongly that I would find Guynemer, and even in Poelcapelle I could see him all the time, "leading" me. But as I went along in the search, I felt less and less close to the conclusion. As this happened, I began to realize I would not find Guynemer at that particular time. It was not in my destiny. I felt certain that I would find him, but not then.

Shortly after the search was officially called off, a leading French newspaper offered to buy the entire Oosterlynck farm so that I could work over it in my own time and do all the digging I wanted. This offer bothered me. I wanted very much to continue the search, but I did not want to work for the press or tie my name to any one newspaper.

Finally, Cora and I went to Ghent to visit M. Jamme and ask his advice. He told us that while we were free to do what we liked in the matter of Guynemer, the French government could not officially associate itself with any search mounted by the press. And so I declined the newspaper's offer. My first hope for the case was to see Guynemer's remains returned to the French people, and to see it done with the proper dignity. I could wait for it because I knew the time would come, sooner or later.

Besides, I had to admit that I was no longer certain that Guynemer's body could be found in that particular field. There was still some aspect of the case I hadn't fully understood. Something was missing.

It wasn't until I left Europe that it all came clear in my mind, and now I believe I know exactly where he is buried. I also know why I did not find him in 1959. It came to me in Australia while I was reading a book about Guynemer, and I learned the fact I hadn't known before.

Contrary to what I thought at the time, the Germans did not bury Guynemer close to the site of his crash. In fact, they moved him quite a distance from the site. They gave him a military funeral with honors, precisely because he was Guynemer. Instead of divining for his remains in Oosterlynck's field, I should have "followed" his funeral.

This was why Guynemer, each time I "saw" him in my mind, seemed to be trying to lead me away.

I am certain I know now exactly where he is. His remains will be identifiable, and I believe I will be able to find him. The case has been uppermost in my mind for almost fifteen years, and even now I am corresponding with the Ministère des Anciens Combattants et Victimes de Guerre in Paris in the hope that when I return to Europe we can conduct another search.

Mrs. Lena Dykshoorn with little Rien in Honselersdijk, Holland, in 1922.

The clairvoyant, left, as hothouse laborer. Dykshoorn's first job was in a hothouse near Honselersdijk, Holland. Note the wooden shoes, or "clogs."

Dykshoorn in the cellar of the shoemaker's shop in Breda, 1948. By clairvoyant divining he apparently followed the course taken by an old priest in the year 1566 and located beneath the cellar floor a metal box that had been buried there for almost four hundred years. (Bernhard van Gils)

This is the Our Lady Church in Breda, Holland, where the search for the sacred Host of Niervaart started.

Rien Dykshoorn, in June 1951, divining by the canal near Sluis, Holland, close to the Belgian border. Here Dykshoorn led police to the submerged body of an old man who had disappeared from a convalescent home.

Dykshoorn at Moerdyk, Holland, in 1954, pinpointing the place where the body of a missing German soldier from World War II would be found. This was done for *Volksbond Deutsche Kriegsgräberürforge.* The remains were exhumed at the exact spot he indicated.

The legendary French World War I pilot, Georges Guynemer, who was shot down during the battle for Flanders in 1917. While searching for the pilot's remains in 1959, Dykshoorn unearthed the remains of seven other servicemen.

Watched by his wife Cora, Rien Dykshoorn divines for human remains in the fields of Poelcapelle, Belgium, in 1959. He found the bodies of seven soldiers killed in the First World War.

Dykshoorn being interviewed by Bob Sanders of ABC television in Sydney, Australia.

The clairvoyant as husband and father. The Dykshoorns in Breda, Holland, in 1958. Pictured with Dykshoorn and his wife Cora is his daughter Helga, then three years old.

Dykshoorn concentrating on a murder site beside the Lane Cove River in Sydney, Australia, where the bodies of a man and woman were found in 1963.

Rien and Cora Dykshoorn in 1965, in Sydney, Australia, where they made their home for almost ten years.

Rien, Cora, and Helga Dykshoorn in Surfers' Paradise, Australia, 1967, with Mrs. Kia Small and her baby, Jamie, whose birth Rien had predicted. Specialists had told Mrs. Small she was incapable of having children. Dykshoorn believed otherwise and told Mrs. Small she would have a baby son thirteen months from the date of her consultation with him.

Dykshoorn at work on a murder case in the United States in 1971, accompanied by James G. Bolton, of Charlotte, North Carolina. Mr. Bolton has accompanied the clairvoyant on several murder cases and, for the benefit of parapsychologists, has prepared detailed affidavits reporting his work.

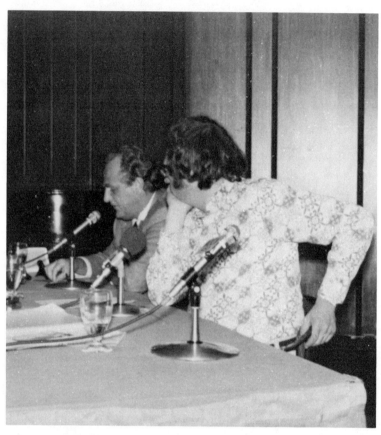

Dykshoorn on radio for three hours with interviewer Larry King in Miami, 1972. After a period of technical questions, listeners who had been clients of Mr. Dykshoorn's called in with stories of the help he had given them.

I I

AUSTRALIA: THE CLAIRVOYANT AS IMMIGRANT

Late in the afternoon of December 17, 1967, Prime Minister of Australia Harold J. Holt disappeared in the sea off Cheviot Beach, near Melbourne in the state of Victoria. Strong and experienced surf swimmer though he was, Mr. Holt dived under a wave in heavy surf and never reappeared.

His disappearance sparked the biggest sea-and-coastal search in the history of the country. The Australian navy and air force as well as police and hundreds of volunteers scoured the coastline and scanned the sea for the prime minister's remains, but no trace of him was found.

I was living in Sydney at that time. On December 20 I decided to offer to help in the search. From our home in the Sydney suburb of Rose Bay I telephoned the home of Mr. L. H. E. Bury, then cabinet minister for Labour and National Service. His home was in the Sydney suburb of Vaucluse, less than a mile from ours. I thought it best to make my offer privately rather than through official channels because I knew the government would not want my involvement publicized in any way.

Mr. Bury was not at home. I was given the number of his office in Parliament House, Canberra, the national capital.

When he finally came on the line, I tried to explain my offer. I genuinely believed I could help find Mr. Holt's body. My record of having assisted European authorities in similar cases could be confirmed by the Dutch embassy in Canberra or the consulate in Sydney.

"I don't expect to be paid," I said. "And I would insist that my search be carried out in complete secrecy. I don't need to know any private or confidential details. I would need only a small boat, reliable maps, and some cooperation from the police. I know my methods sound very unusual, but if you will make a small boat available to me, I believe I can lead the skindivers to Mister Holt's body."

Mr. Bury was polite and receptive. He promised to discuss the matter with the federal cabinet and phone me the following day with the decision.

Two days later I telephoned his home again. Mr. Bury had gone on vacation to the mountains and could not be reached.

By January 2, 1968, Mr. Holt's body still had not been found. A Sydney newspaper published a map of that section of the coast showing where the search efforts were being concentrated.

I worked over this map with the divining wire and became convinced Mr. Holt's body was not in the area being so thoroughly searched. My gift also indicated to me exactly where the body was. I had recently completed a course in navigation, and so I was able to plot the exact location of the spot, to the nearest degree. The body was still in the sea on January 2; it had not been devoured by sharks, as was being widely supposed.

I telephoned Vaucluse again and spoke to Mr. Bury. He told me the cabinet had decided it could not justify expending public money to sponsor a search for Mr. Holt by psychic means.

Hundreds of searchers including the armed forces had been scouring the area for more than two weeks. A small boat could not be made available for one day.

"It is not necessary for me to visit the scene," I said. "I have a map and I have worked it out here at home. I just want to pass on to you my belief that the skindivers are searching in the wrong area and that I can indicate exactly where Minister Holt can be found. I am a certified navigator and I have plotted the exact location. What harm can it do to send someone to look there?"

At this point Mr. Bury became brusque. He said he did not wish to discuss the matter further, and he hung up.

Mr. Holt's body, of course, was never found.

I have already said that only occasionally does my psychic ability permit me to foretell events in my own life. If it had in 1960, and if I had been able to see how things would be in Australia, I probably would not have looked forward with much enthusiasm to the next ten years of my life—especially since I believe that if I foresee something happening through my psychic gift, it will happen, regardless of what the person does to try and prevent it.

The story of our decade-long sojourn in Australia is, unhappily, mostly one of disappointment, frustration, and wasted opportunities. We loved the country and we loved the people and I managed to establish a successful and satisfying practice in Sydney, but the major cases did not come my way.

In Australia I worked on no case comparable in importance or significance to the search for Guynemer, the search for the Host of Niervaart, or the *"telefonvision"* cases. And in particular, I was denied the police cases that had so sustained and satisfied me in Europe.

I tried. Time and time again I offered my services to the police and the state and federal governments, but I was simply not *allowed* to work on police cases. At every turning I met the closed doors of stereotyped bureaucratic thinking. My offers were greeted with indifference and, I suppose, disdain. No one in a position of authority bothered to check my past record, even in the face of what amounted to pleading by myself and friends who tried to intercede on my behalf.

My record of having helped the police forces of western Europe could have been verified with a telephone call, but we could persuade no one to entertain the possibility even to that extent. Sadly, the story of my fruitless attempt to help locate the drowned body of the prime minister was repeated in other cases, and many of those cases involved the unsolved murders of children.

Why did we leave Europe at all, and especially in 1960, so shortly after my most successful and widely publicized case? The answer is: precisely *because* things were going so well.

No doubt if we had stayed in Holland, my family and I could have enjoyed a life of comfort, prosperity, and position in the community. But it was not enough. In Europe, and especially in the Netherlands, ESP had become widely accepted. Research programs had taken hold in the universities and the authorities had demonstrated their willingness to put the proven abilities of psychic people to practical use. ESP had become respectable.

In other parts of the world, however, psychic matters had not gained such wide acceptance. The interest was there, but the few genuine psychics had never been able to overcome the dubious reputation that had accrued to the field in general. Most people's natural skepticism had been fanned by the transparently fraudulent activities of the charlatans and the self-deluding practitioners of the so-called "occult" or "black arts" who claimed to use ESP in their dubious and often devious work.

Even parapsychology itself was regarded as a somewhat nefarious fringe activity, less than a science and only slightly above the level of superstition. Although many people were prepared to accept ESP as a concept or possibility, people claiming to be "psychic" were seldom taken seriously.

This was a situation I felt obliged to try and correct, as far as my capabilities allowed. I believe in predestination, and I knew that my gift would take me away from western Europe and into the wider world, lecturing and demonstrating until as many people as I could reach started getting the message: ESP is real, ESP is a human faculty; it works, it can be used, it can be very valuable. Even though it meant abandoning my successful practice in Europe and placing the future security of my family in jeopardy, I knew I had to go.

But why Australia? Cora would have preferred the United States, where at least some serious parapsychological research was being done, but I did not feel ready for America. I knew we would have to go there eventually, but I would wait until we had gained at least a reasonable command of English.

Also, I had become fascinated with the prospect of Australia. Here was an enormous country, a young nation, English-speaking, democratic, its small population thinly spread over a vast continent subject to a benevolent climate, its economy already buoyant and poised on the brink of an era of fabulous wealth.

I thought, too, that I might be able to contribute something valuable to the country in its quest for expansion. For most of its history, Australia had been an agricultural country, but by 1960 the people had begun to find wealth beneath their feet. under the ground—minerals, ores, precious stones, oil, and natural gas, vital resources that would drastically alter the course of their march into the future. And I was a diviner; could I not help to locate deposits of these natural resources? I thought so.

And so, Australia it was. We flew from The Hague on December 30, 1960, on the inaugural KLM flight direct to Sydney, and thirty-six hours later we were in Sydney, sweltering in the 90-degree heat of an Australian New Year's Day. Our life as an immigrant family had begun.

As a matter of fact, it was not all bad. In time we settled happily into our new way of life. From a succession of apartments we moved into a beautiful home overlooking a golf course and Sydney's magnificent harbor, and gradually I was able to build up a clientele. I began lecturing, first to Dutch immigrant groups, and then, as my English improved, to Australian audiences.

But it was not long before we encountered the bureaucratic

attitudes and narrow-minded modes of thinking that were to stand in our way as long as we remained in Australia.

My hopes of finding oil or minerals by psychic divining were quickly put down, although it seemed for a while that these plans might be quickly brought to fruition.

In the wake of an article in the *Dutch-Australian Weekly*, a fellow immigrant offered me my first chance of using my gift to search for underground wealth.

"Come with me to Coober Pedy," he said. A few weeks later he and I set out for one of the strangest communities in the world.

Coober Pedy is a township founded on opal mining, a remote outpost in the desolate wasteland of central Australia. To escape the searing heat of the desert sun the inhabitants live under the ground, in cavelike dwellings that are actually well-equipped homes. Only the doorways show above ground, so that driving into the settlement one sees only so many little wooden structures like outhouses, and mounds of earth with doorways leading into them.

Not surprisingly, a large percentage of the population at any given time consists of itinerant prospectors and transients.

Contrary to popular belief, very few high-quality stones are found on the surface, especially in areas where prospectors and tourists have been coming and going and turning over rocks for years.

My companion and I stayed in Coober Pedy eight weeks, in 120-degree temperatures, mining a claim fifty feet square. We did find opals, but most of them were low-quality quartz crystals. We dug our claim to a depth of about ten feet, but my gift told me there were no high-quality stones there and, of course, we could not dig beyond the boundaries of our own claim.

Still, I was encouraged. Most of the stones we did find, I had located with the divining rod, proving to my satisfaction that my gift could be used for that purpose.

Back in Sydney I began offering my services directly to the

mining companies that held leases over practically all the potentially rich mining areas of the continent.

Perhaps inevitably, I found no takers. The possibility that oil, minerals, or precious stones might be located by psychic means was simply too "way out" for the mining company executives, despite the fact that costs would have been negligible and the benefits potentially enormous. I encountered only skepticism, indifference, and amusement, and I was shown the door of many a plush office.

Finally I resigned myself to the probability that I would never divine for oil or minerals in Austrailia.

Then in late 1961 came another disappointment. A weekly magazine, *PIX,* having heard of my work for the police in Europe, suggested an article linking my name with an unsolved murder case. They promised to provide, in an unsensational manner, details of some of my European work along with a quote that I was anxious to help in this particular case.

I was against it at first. I would not work on any case without the full knowledge and cooperation of the police. But then I became genuinely interested in the case itself and I agreed to the article. It couldn't do any harm to bring my past record to the attention of the police.

The murder in question had remained unsolved for a year. Dr. James Macrae Yeates, a prominent Sydney doctor, was found dead in the garage of his home. He was first thought to have died from an accidental electric shock, but a postmortem revealed that his skull had been fractured and his heart punctured by a hypodermic syringe.

The *PIX* article, when it appeared, hinted that I had already "worked out" the case and was anxious to pass on my knowledge to the police. But the police did not react to it. Then when I tried to offer my services directly to the police, I was turned down.

On the credit side, my English was improving, clients had started coming regularly for consultations, and I had started giving lectures. The pattern of our life in Australia had begun to take form.

12

MEASURES OF DISAPPOINTMENT

On New Year's Day, 1963, the seminaked bodies of Dr. Gilbert Bogle and Mrs. Margaret Chandler were found alongside Dr. Bogle's car on the banks of the Lane Cove River, in a green-belt area of surburban Sydney. The case of their apparent murder is one of the most puzzling in the annals of crime.

The cause of death was never established. There were no signs of a struggle, no marks on the bodies, no traces of drugs or poison. Although the case is popularly referred to as the Bogle–Chandler Murder Case, it has never been established whether it was double murder or double suicide.

From the moment this case broke, it was tailor-made for a psychic investigation. What had happened on the river bank in the early hours of New Year's morning? I knew that by visiting the site and concentrating on the dead people, I could reconstruct everything that took place; I had done it before, many times.

It was obvious that the police would not ask for my assistance, as the police in Europe had done in similar cases, so I knew I had to take it upon myself to offer my services.

I asked a friend to intercede on my behalf with the then chief of the Criminal Investigation Branch of the New South Wales Police, Superintendent R. J. Walden. However, the officer displayed no interest in my offer and declined even to meet with me.

On January 26 I wrote to Superintendent Walden to explain my offer. I referred to the Dutch embassy, the Netherlands Department of Justice in The Hague, and the Faculty of Paranormal Phenomena at the University of Utrecht, at any one of which he could have checked my credentials and past record of having materially assisted police forces in Europe.

To my pleasure—and somewhat to my surprise—Superintendent Walden's reply was cautiously encouraging. Exactly how, he asked, did I believe I could assist in the case?

I replied at length. I wished to visit the Lane Cove River bank in the company of a policeman, and I would try to describe what had happened to Dr. Bogle and Mrs. Chandler. Then I would try to follow the route the murderer took on his way from the scene of the crime to his home. I insisted that I should work entirely without publicity, nor would I need to know any confidential information about the case. I would merely try to provide the police with a theory about the case, from which they might be able to gather evidence.

Finally, I stated: "I should like to assist in this matter not only for reasons of security, but also to provide interesting material for those universities in Europe and the United States which spend so much time and money on parapsychological research."

Superintendent Walden replied: "The reasons you advance do not provide me with any grounds to justify my seeking your aid in the investigation. Therefore, I can see no useful purpose served in granting your request."

I was stunned. This was my first encounter with the type of attitude that could not see any justification for making one police officer available for several hours on the possibility that a case of murder might be solved. There was no expense involved, nor any chance that the police might have been embarrassed by publicity. It was, or should have been, a classic situation of having nothing to lose and everything to gain.

But there was nothing I could do. My offer was rejected, and that was that.

Meanwhile, after a full decade of fruitless police investigation of the Bogle–Chandler case by conventional methods, the case remains as mysterious as it was the morning the bodies were found. Not even the cause of death has ever been established.

I tried again, several times over the next few years, but the New South Wales police were immovable in their indifference. I wrote, telephoned, and tried to obtain personal interviews with senior officers, but not once could I persuade any of them to take my offers seriously enough even to check my credentials. The situation looked hopeless.

Then suddenly, in 1967, it seemed that I was going to be allowed to work on a case for the Australian police.

On January 26, 1966, three children of the Beaumont family— Jane, nine, Arrna, seven, and Grant, four—disappeared without trace from Glenelg Beach, near Adelaide in the state of South Australia. Nothing had been seen or heard of them since.

In early 1967 another Dutch psychic claimed, in Holland, to have seen a "vision" of the missing children. According to his "vision," they were buried under a building in Adelaide.

This claim caused a storm of controversy in Australia, especially since it had never been established that the children were dead, and their parents, naturally, still held hopes that they were alive.

An Adelaide citizens' group raised funds from public contributions to bring this psychic to Australia to conduct a search. He was not to work for the police, but only for the citizens' group that paid him.

A great deal of digging was done, but no trace of the Beaumont children was found.

In January, 1967, I offered my services secretly to the South

Australian police. I did not believe the other psychic would find the children, and I asked permission to investigate the case in my own way.

"I don't know what happened to the children," I said. "But I believe I can find out."

Surprisingly enough, in view of my experiences with the New South Wales police, the Adelaide police were cautiously receptive.

"We don't mind if you come to Adelaide," they said, "and we will help you all we can, but everything must be done in complete secrecy. We don't want it known we are accepting advice from a clairvoyant. Clairvoyants aren't too popular in this part of the world right now."

"Well, that is the way I want it, too," I said.

Cora and I drove to Adelaide, more than a thousand miles from Sydney, and met with one of the detectives investigating the case. Together we drove around the streets of suburban Adelaide for about two hours while I familiarized myself with the terrain. I worked on the case only in a very preliminary way, but at no time did we leave the car to start a search.

"I will have to come back to conduct a thorough search," I told the detectives. "It may take several days and I will need full co-operation from the police so that I can go wherever my gift leads me. You understand I may have to pass over private property or go into buildings, so I must have your authority backing me up."

The detective said that he would have to get permission for the search to be carried out, and that he would let us know by mail. Cora and I went back to Sydney to wait.

Then about six weeks later I received a telephone call from a Melbourne newspaper, *The Truth*. The reporter said that the police were digging in the Adelaide Hills for the bodies of the Beaumont children and that I was supposed to have told them where to dig!

I was flabbergasted! "I know nothing about it," I told him, because I wanted to protect the parents of the children and maintain my pledge of secrecy to the police.

"But we know you were in Adelaide last month. The police have confirmed it."

The following morning, this story appeared in *The Truth* under the banner: SECRET DIG BY POLICE

> . . . The police dig follows information they received from a second Dutch clairvoyant. . . . Mr. M. B. Dykshoorn visited Adelaide last month. He told police the Beaumonts had been kidnapped by a pervert, murdered and buried in the Adelaide Hills. . . . Mr. Dykshoorn gave police the description of a man. Police . . . acted on Mr. Dykshoorn's advice. Several men were detailed to go quietly to a certain spot in the Adelaide Hills. . . . The dig has revealed no new clue so far.

Naturally the story was picked up by other newspapers. It was patently obvious there had been a leak from the police in Adelaide, yet this did not worry me as much as the news that the police had been digging at a site I had supposedly indicated. Never at any stage had we left the car in Adelaide, and certainly I had never pointed out any place to dig. It was unthinkable that I would have gone away from Adelaide leaving them to dig alone. I would have to be there, on the spot.

But I kept my mouth shut and refused to comment to the press. Anything I might have said would have contradicted the police, who were clearly using me as a scapegoat. Besides, I still hoped that if I kept my part of the agreement with the police, I might be allowed to return to Adelaide and complete my investigation once the furor died down.

These hopes, however, were dashed when the very detective with whom I had worked on the case, Detective-Inspector Eaton, told the *Sydney Daily Mirror*: "I have been in contact with Mr. Dykshoorn and have sent him a report on the digging."

Of course, I never received any such report, or any other communication from Detective-Inspector Eaton. Nor was I ever allowed to return to Adelaide to conduct a proper search for the Beaumont children, who remain missing to this day.

People often ask me why, if I think I can help in a murder case or find a body, I don't work it out for myself and then go to the police with my information or, if I find it, the body. The reason is that the worst thing that can happen to me is to start on a case and then not be able to finish it. It gets inside me, it occupies me. I become emotionally involved and I identify very strongly with the people—the killers as well as the victims. I don't know them personally, but they are very real people to me.

If I start a case, but cannot finish it, it places a terrible strain on me. I *need* to finish it. I get very distraught and very emotionally upset, and it's a situation I can't risk going through too often.

This is why I will work only for the police, with their full knowledge and cooperation. I can't work for families, or individuals, or insurance companies, or private investigators, or anyone other than the police, because once I start on a case, I must not be stopped by outside intervention. It's impossible for me.

Whenever someone asks me to work on such a case, I always tell them to go to the police and ask the police to come to me. If the police are agreeable, then I will do it, but otherwise, I can't get involved. It's too dangerous for me, personally. And then when I do work on a criminal case, I will give my information only to the police, who may use it in any way they see fit.

Twice in Australia I was allowed to start work on a case, then cut off before I could complete my work. The first time was in the Beaumont children case, the second time was in April, 1967.

The case was known as the Wanda Beach Murders. The bodies of two fifteen-year-old girls, Marrianne Schmidt and Christine Sharrock, were found partially buried in the sand dunes on Wanda Beach, south of Sydney, on January 11, 1965. Both girls had been savagely beaten and stabbed. By 1967, the police had come up with no solid lead on the case.

One day in April, Cora and I went alone to Wanda Beach, and

I concentrated on the murders. I saw what happened and I saw the killer. He came into me and I was able to feel his raging urge to kill. I knew that he was an uncontrollable psychopath, another dangerously violent schizophrenic capable of "flipping" into a murderous frame of mind.

I became very upset. My own daughter, Helga, was twelve years old. This was one case I *needed* to see through to its conclusion.

I phoned the Sydney CIB and this time was granted an interview with a Sergeant Douglas at a suburban station. He agreed to accompany me to Wanda Beach and a week later we went there together.

I concentrated on the killer, and immediately I found myself hunched over, walking in a half-crippled, shuffling gait.

"He walks like this when he is aroused," I said. "He reacts to things he sees that upset the balance of his mind and he becomes crazed. He is a schizophrenic. Yet when he calms down he walks normally. Nobody would know he is the same man. Not from the way he walks."

Then I began "following" the killer. I was going to walk wherever he had walked that day after murdering the two girls.

From the beach we made our way through the streets and a nearby suburban shopping center until we came to the entrance of a social club. The killer had gone inside.

"I must go in," I said.

But the sergeant balked. "I don't know," he said. "We don't want anyone to know about this, and I'm not authorized to take you inside."

"But I must go inside!" I said. "The killer went in that day. Someone may have seen him. The people who work here. He was behaving very strangely that day, walking like this. They might remember——"

"I will have to let you know, Mister Dykshoorn," he said. "I was told to observe and report back. We will have to quit now, but I will keep you informed."

And that, of course, was that. I never received any further communication from Sergeant Douglas, and despite countless telephone calls to officers from the police commissioner down, I never again worked on the Wanda Beach Murders.

Friends in Australia tell me that the case has now been solved. I only wish I could have helped solve it sooner.

13

SUCCESS IN THE PRIVATE SECTOR

One thing that came out of all this trouble with the Australian police was a determination to build a weight of evidence in support of my gift and my work. In Europe we had never bothered to gather documentary proof of my work in any systematic way, because no one, from the government down, ever seriously questioned the fact that I was genuinely psychic. If anyone had, I would simply have referred them to the police or to the universities at which I had been tested and found to be *bona fide,* or to the press reports of my lectures and various major cases.

Naturally we had kept a file of newspaper clippings, and I had retained such documents as notary Robert Batten's statement testifying to my recovery of the rixdollars in Middelburg, but it never occurred to us that we might need more proof of the validity of my psychic talents.

In Australia we found that my European work counted for nothing, and as my relations with the authorities degenerated almost into antagonism, I suddenly found myself in a potentially vulnerable situation.

Technically, it was against the law to practice clairvoyance in the state of New South Wales, or to "profess to tell the future for financial reward." True, the law was seldom if ever enforced, but as I was continually in personal contact with senior police officers, some of my Australian friends began to worry about my situation under this law.

"If you offend someone in a high place," they said, "you might find the police choosing to enforce this law in your case. They might find it a convenient way of keeping you from making waves in their pond."

So because the law banned *professing* to tell the future, Cora and I set about assembling a file of documentary proof that I really *could* predict future events in the lives of others—proof that would stand up in court if the need arose.

We did this by asking some of my clients to prepare legally binding affidavits—"statutory declarations" in Australia—testifying to some of the work I had done for them in the area of predicting future events. An affidavit is, of course, a legally binding document signed under oath and is admissible as evidence in any court.

Not that we asked all my clients to help out in this way, or made it a condition of a private consultation. My work for clients is done in the strictest confidence, and I am not so naive as to believe that all my clients would like it known that they seek advice from a clairvoyant. Besides, it takes times for any prediction of the future to be realized, and many of my clients leave my office emphatically not believing that what I have told them will happen, will really happen. The only reliable affidavit comes from the person who comes back after something I have predicted has come to pass.

To the people who did prepare such affidavits on my behalf, I am deeply grateful. They did so in the knowledge that their names might one day be revealed in public as having sought the advice of a clairvoyant, and in certain climates of opinion, that takes courage.

As it happened, I was never prosecuted in Australia under the "fortune-telling" law, but I am nonetheless grateful to my Australian clients. When the time came to prepare this book, we asked their permission to use their names and statements to verify that I can in fact foretell future events, and not one of them turned us down.

Mr. Leslie Horvath, of 133 New South Head Road, Sydney, prepared this affidavit:

> In August 1968 my car was stolen and the police were unable to locate it. I consulted Mr. Dykshoorn, clairvoyant, whom I had consulted about seven years ago. Many of the predictions he had made for me had come to pass, so I thought he might be able to help locate my car.
> Mr. Dykshoorn told me my car had been stolen by criminals who were using it for robberies, etc. He predicted that it would be found by the police between ten and fifteen days hence, in the western suburbs of Sydney. He said there would be definite evidence that it had been used in robberies.
> It was found thirteen days later in the western suburbs. The car was fitted with false license plates and had obviously been used by criminals.
> I am a committee member of the Vizor Club [a Sydney businessmen's club] and told the other members about this prediction at least ten days before the car was found. All these people can testify to the proof of this statement.

Jacob Gobes, a well-known Sydney restaurateur and caterer, became a good friend despite the fact that I made some not-so-cheerful predictions about the future of his business—and despite the fact that he ignored them.

We met when a mutual friend took Core and me to Jacob's Tulips restaurant in downtown Sydney. The moment we walked into the place I felt something disastrous was going to happen there, so I took out my divining rod and concentrated on the problem.

When we were introduced to Jacob, I said: "This is a nice place, but I have to tell you it's going to be burnt out twice."

Jacob didn't know I was psychic. He said: "Don't be silly."

Two and a half years later the Tulips was engulfed by fire. Jacob came to me and said: "Well, I hope you're happy now!"

"Of course, I'm not happy," I said. "But I told you it would happen and I'm telling you now it will happen again."

Eight months later the Tulips was again burned down.

Jacob was good enough to testify to these predictions in an affidavit:

> On another occasion Mr. Dykshoorn visited a restaurant of which I was the proprietor and told me that the following day the chair in which he was sitting would be occupied by my first employer. I doubted this for two reasons: firstly because that particular place was occupied every day at lunchtime by a regular customer; secondly because my first job had been at an hotel in Holland when I was thirteen years old and I could not even remember the name of my employer at the time.
>
> The following day my regular customer brought a guest to lunch, although he sat in his usual place. Then suddenly the two men changed places, so that the guest occupied the chair Mr. Dykshoorn had nominated. I was later introduced to the guest, who, after learning my name, said he had been the manager of the hotel in Amsterdam when I had worked there. . . .
>
> On yet another occasion about five years ago, Mr. Dykshoorn told me that I would work for a large company in a circular building in Sydney, although at the time I was entirely self-employed and had no intention of changing that situation. Mr. Dykshoorn further told me in some detail the nature of the catering work I would supervise in my future employment.
>
> I now manage a catering business in the circular tower in Sydney known as the Australia Square Tower. The nature of my work is almost exactly as Mr. Dykshoorn described. It is remarkable that at the time Mr. Dykshoorn made his prediction, the Australia Square [building] project had not been commenced or even announced. (See Appendix.)

Some of my clients want to know what will happen in their businesses or careers, others are worried over personal or family problems. Architect John Egan, of the Sydney suburb of Ryde, was concerned over the future of his son.

> I consulted Mr. M. B. Dykshoorn, clairvoyant, in October 1968. He told me of my early life and family problems with amazing accuracy. He described the personalities of my family and made certain predictions for the future.
>
> The most amazing prediction concerned my eighteen-year-old son who had left home about eighteen months before to work in the country. I was rather worried about this boy as he never wrote to us. Mr. Dykshoorn told me not to worry as the boy would soon be joining the army and this would make a man of him.
>
> I found this rather hard to believe as the boy could not be drafted for another two years and he did not seem the type of boy who would voluntarily join the army. I was sure this would not happen.
>
> However, about a week later I received a letter from the boy, and attached to this letter was an application form to join the army, which required my signature.
>
> The boy is now in the army as Mr. Dykshoorn predicted.

Ian Hay, a young Sydney businessman, became a regular client in the late sixties. He tells his own story better than I probably could:

> I first saw Mr. Dykshoorn at a lecture he gave at the Vizor Club. At that time I knew nothing about clairvoyance or ESP, but I was astounded by what I saw. As a result, I made an appointment for a personal consultation with him.
>
> On the day of my appointment I had a long business discussion with my bank manager. When I arrived at Mr. Dykshoorn's home, he amazed me by telling me of my discussion with the bank manager, describing the business we had discussed, and he told me, to the cent, the amounts involved.
>
> He also told me of my feelings on personal matters which I cannot discuss here. The points which he "saw" and which I can discuss are as follows:
>
> 1. He told me I have five men working in my business. Correct.

2. He gave details of my family, number of children, approximate ages and personalities. He was uncannily accurate in this.
3. One of my businesses is a food-processing factory. He drew a plan of the layout, giving details of specialized equipment and its approximate position on the floor. He was correct in almost every detail.
4. He told me that the profits from my concrete business were carrying the losses of the food business. This was correct.
5. The most interesting prediction was as follows: He foresaw my buying a chicken processing business in an area close to Hunter's Hill, a suburb of Sydney. He told me this business would specialize in taking the bones out of chickens. I was amused by this, as I knew of no type of business which bones out chickens.

The following Friday I was talking to a friend about the purchase of some refrigeration equipment I needed. This friend told me of a business which was in difficulties and had some equipment to sell. . . . To my amazement it was a chicken factory at Eastwood (near Hunter's Hill), and it specialized in boning out chickens to supply chicken meat to Chinese restaurants!

This was the first time I ever knew that this type of business existed. In fact, as far as I know, it is the only business of its type in Sydney. I would like to make it clear that I did not set out to find such a business. I stumbled over it while looking for something completely different. However, it turned up in my life exactly as Mr. Dykshoorn said it would. So far I have avoided going to see this business for fear I might be tempted to buy it!

Before my first visit to Mr. Dykshoorn, I was arranging a deal to purchase a concrete pumping machine to supplement my existing concrete business. I did not mention this on my first visit because I was too astounded by other things he told me. However, in the weeks following I decided to pay Mr. Dykshoorn another visit.

Discussing the concrete pump, Mr. Dykshoorn said: "Forget it. You will work for nothing and you will lose money. Forget it."

On December 1, 1968, I took delivery of the pump for

$22,000, against Mr. Dykshoorn's advice. The first job was a complete success. This was a test job for a large building company, done at no charge, as a demonstration. The manager booked the pump for the following Tuesday, at Rose Bay.

As I passed Mr. Dykshoorn's home on my way to the job, my thoughts flashed back to our conversation and I remembered he had advised me not to buy the pump. I talked myself into believing that he might have been right in the past, but he was probably wrong sometimes. This would be all right.

At 12.30 P.M., disaster struck. The pump blew a high pressure oil line—$160 worth of concrete wasted, overtime for eight men. The job finished at 8 P.M. at a cost of $300 to my company.

The next job was on Thursday 12. Disaster struck again; this time a bill for $600. On Friday 13, more trouble. On the job at 4.30 A.M., finished at 6.30 P.M. Total losses for this job as yet unknown. It will probably be at least $400.

The first week's trading losses were about $2,500. Other troubles followed, and after discussions with my accountant I have decided to get out of the concrete pumping business. Again Mr. Dykshoorn was right.

I do not go about trying to make his predictions come true, but they seem to happen just the same.

Mrs. Kia Small, from the Queensland resort town of Surfers' Paradise, came to me for a private consultation in 1964. Like many other women before and since, she wanted to know if she would ever have a baby.

I concentrated on her and saw that indeed she would, so I said: "Yes, you will have a baby boy about thirteen months from now."

As far as I was concerned there was nothing unusual about the case, but then she told me that specialists had told her she would never be able to bear children.

"Well, I don't know," I said. "I can only tell you what I see through my gift, and I see a boy about thirteen months from now."

We heard no more about it until April, 1967, when Cora, Helga, and I went to Surfers' Paradise on vacation. Mrs. Small heard we were coming to town and she took her story to the *Gold Coast Bulletin*: "Although I had a great deal of confidence in Mr. Dykshoorn," she said, "I must admit I couldn't bring myself to believe that he was right and the specialists were wrong.

"But he was right. I did have a baby boy as he predicted. And by the time my baby came my faith in Mr. Dykshoorn's power was completely restored, even to the extent of having only blue-for-a-boy clothes for the arrival."

Then, to follow up the story, the *Gold Coast Bulletin* sent a reporter named Kelvene Shipman to interview me at our motel, and I worked for her.

This is what she wrote:

> . . . Mr. Dykshoorn began my story. As he walked up and down he used a piece of wire, similar to a divining rod, gripping it with both hands.
>
> This, he explained, has nothing to do with the sixth sense, but merely helps his concentration.
>
> I smiled at the drama of the situation, but within three minutes I had completely changed my mind.
>
> Without any effort Mr. Dykshoorn told me of our family history, the places I had lived and worked in, described various people I knew well, even to the point of showing me how they walked and sat.
>
> Having dealt with the past he went on to discuss my future and I'm just glad everything is going to work out so happily.
>
> He was so dead right about the past I think it would worry me to death if he had made any dire predictions for the future.
>
> That was it! I went in a disbeliever and came away stupefied at what I had seen and heard.

Along the same lines, the leading Sydney columnist Ron Saw wrote of his experiences with me in the Sydney *Sunday Telegraph* on August 4, 1968:

> . . . When I had settled on a sofa in a small, sparsely furnished room, he pulled a loop of wire from his pocket,

rather like a doctor producing a stethoscope, twirled and frowned, and began pacing.

"Do you know or recall," he said, "someone who walks like this?"

I was ready for it, but still it startled me. It was, to the very last movement, the busy, slightly duck-footed gait of my father.

"No," I said defiantly.

He frowned and twirled the wire again. "I see it," he said. "Your father? Yes, your father. I'm sure. Your father had a bad leg. Knee . . . he hurt his knee playing some sport, and it always gave him trouble, but he played a lot of sport after he hurt his knee."

I exhaled gustily. My father did, in fact, wreck his knee playing football. But later he was a state cricketer, a plus-two golfer and a lawn-bowls champion.

"Oh, all right," I said. "Yes."

The work I did for another client in Australia was to follow us to America. In 1967 Mrs. Leigh Bonheur came to me. She was then an aspiring writer.

In June, 1971, while we were living in Charlotte, North Carolina, Mrs. Bonheur wrote me a letter enclosing the following testimonial, which she indicated I may show to anyone:

Some four years ago Mr. Dykshoorn told me that the book I had just written "would not be accepted for a long time." Which was so. He also told me that when it was accepted "it would be published under a three-word title and that the title would become a generic term for the type of child the book is about."

The publisher, Ure Smith, named the book *Hand Me Down* just one hour before sending the MS to the printer, and already the title is being used as a descriptive phrase concerning unwanted or illegitimate children.

Mr. Dykshoorn also said that it would be a "best seller," which it has been—the first edition of 5,000 hard-back copies selling out within three weeks of publication and it is now in its third edition.

Along with her testimonial, Leigh Bonheur sent us a critic's review of her book describing it as "brilliant and arresting," and a newspaper's list of best sellers in Australia. *Hand Me Down* was sixth in the nonfiction list.

See additional testimonials in Appendix.

14

AMERICA: A NEW BEGINNING

We were frustrated in Australia. Our life there was very happy and
pleasant and I was very successful in my practice; the press and
media were kind to me; my lectures were always well received and
my clients—many more of whom supplied adavits than those few
we have reported here—went out of their way to help and support
us; but finally it became obvious that we were never going to make
any headway with the police or other authorities.

Not that the police can be blamed for not being aware of the
possibilities of ESP and psychic abilities. Even the academic and
scientific community in Australia was almost totally unaware of
what has been achieved in the field of parapsychology in recent
years. There were no departments of parapsychology at the universities, nor did the scientific community display the slightest interest in the subject.

Once I was asked to appear on a television program for the
Australian Broadcasting Commission. In a filmed interview I told
of cases I had worked on in Europe, bodies I had found and so on,
and showed a newspaper clipping which stated unequivocally that
I had found seven human skeletons while searching for Guynemer.

Then three prominent scientists held a panel discussion on ESP. One said he hadn't enough knowledge of the field to comment; another said that some kind of research should be undertaken; and the third said that psychic people always seemed a little "screwy."

Of course, none of these scientists had even the slightest familiarity with ESP or parapsychology. They were not aware of any of the research that has been going on for almost half a century, and since no one had ever shown them that ESP can be useful, they knew nothing about it at all.

Things have been quite different here in America. Naturally we have encountered skepticism and indifference and even hostility from individuals, but this has been the case all our lives and we are used to it. Generally, the American people have been very receptive, fair, open-minded, and surprisingly knowledgeable about ESP and its possibilities. We have lived in three different cities—Charlotte, North Carolina, Miami, and New York—and we have done a lot of traveling for lectures and important cases, and everywhere we have found people to be genuinely interested in what I do.

It is part of the American tradition, of course, to be receptive to new ideas and to treat each case and claim on its merits. Nevertheless, Cora and I could not be happier with our reception here. The audiences at my lectures have been knowledgeable, responsive, and perceptive; clients have come to me from as far afield as Oregon, Texas, California, Vermont, and even Canada; universities, colleges, and high schools have invited me to lecture and discuss my abilities with students who display a keen and level-headed interest in parapsychology; the police on the six occasions I have worked for them on murder cases have been cooperative, understanding, and patient; and even the American press—the toughest-minded and best-informed in the world—has been kind to me.

Twice I have been appointed an associate member of the Sheriff's Association of North Carolina—for my work in cooperation with the police of that state—and in 1971 the then governor of Kentucky, Louis B. Nunn, commissioned me a Kentucky colonel "in consideration of outstanding achievement." Could it happen anywhere else in the world that a man claiming to be psychic, and nothing else, should be so honored?

I have a theory about Americans and their attitude toward ESP—one that runs contrary to a popular notion of sociologists and those who analyze the collective psyche of this nation's two hundred million people. At various times I have read that American interest in ESP "ebbs and flows as the people feel the need to believe in some power or force beyond what they can see in the real world"—or words to this effect. I disagree. I never ask people to "believe in" anything, but only to witness what I do, examine the facts, and determine the value in their own minds. The majority of American people are realists—you cannot tell an American what to believe; he will believe what he chooses to believe, regardless of what you say.

But facts are something else. Show an American that you can do something useful and valuable and he will respect you for being able to do it. And so I am convinced that the reason many Americans believe in ESP is not that the belief fills a need to put faith in something beyond reality, but that people in this country are becoming increasingly aware that ESP is a *part* of reality. ESP exists, psychic phenomena occur and can be seen to occur. Only by stripping the mystery away from the field can we come closer to grasping the realities of ESP, and achieving a better understanding of ourselves.

We came to the United States in April, 1970. Our reasons for leaving Australia are obvious, yet we had a particular reason for arriving when we did.

I came to have my psychic abilities tested and examined by the best-known and most respected researcher into parapsychology in the world—Dr. J. B. Rhine of the Institute for Parapsychology in Durham, North Carolina.

My correspondence with Dr. Rhine had begun in 1967, and,

though I had often been disappointed in Europe with the methods of parapsychologists, I was expecting to have a fruitful relationship with Dr. Rhine. An Australian friend traveling in the United States had shown him some of the documentation relating to my work, and Dr. Rhine had written that he was "definitely favorable" toward an undertaking to study my abilities. He hoped to move his own research work in the direction of possible applications for ESP, he wrote, and a project along these lines might be based on my past work.

Dr. Rhine had won recognition and respect for his pioneering work in establishing that a psychic faculty does exist in human beings, and that most, if not all of us, possess extrasensory perception to a greater or lesser degree. For more than forty years, first in the Parapsychology Laboratory at Duke University and later at his independently constituted Institute for Parapsychology, Dr. Rhine had been subjecting people to statistical tests and had determined beyond reasonable doubt that many apparently "normal" people are able to score very highly indeed in such tests. As a result, he had been able to impress upon the scientific world and the world in general that the concept of extrasensory perception has a basis in reality.

For my own part, I had always respected Dr. Rhine's accomplishments—even though I had argued strongly with researchers who had tried to use exactly the same methods to test my abilities—and I felt obliged to volunteer to undergo an examination at his institute. If Dr. Rhine now felt ready to explore areas of practical application for psychic abilities, I was willing to make myself available in Durham.

In 1970 Dr. Rhine had written to me, indicating that he would be open to any suggestions I might make that might lead to a useful test of my capacities, "particularly in the direction of application to human affairs."

This was what we had been waiting for. We set to packing again, and when we set out for America our destination was Durham, North Carolina.

On the way, however, we encountered a curious and almost farcical situation in California.

We had thought, given a choice, we might like to live in California, somewhere near Los Angeles, where our friend from Australia had business contacts who might help us settle.

The day after our arrival we went to dinner with our friend, who brought along as a guest a commissioner of police from the Los Angeles area—and he dropped a bombshell.

"I have to tell you, Mister Dykshoorn," he said, "that you can't practice as a clairvoyant in California unless you have yourself ordained as a minister of religion."

At first we thought he was joking, but he was not. Section 43.30 of the Los Angeles Municipal Code prohibits "fortune-telling" which, like the Australian law, it defines as "professing to reveal future events in the lives of others." However, Section 43.31 says that "fortune-telling" is legal if it is done by an "accredited minister" of any religion.

I was astounded! Apparently it was illegal to practice clairvoyance as an ordinary person, but if you had yourself ordained as an "accredited minister" of any religion—even one you invented for yourself—you could do just about anything you chose and the law couldn't touch you. Under Section 43.31, you would be exempt from the provisions of Section 43.30.

"But that's ridiculous!" I said. "This is a law with a built-in loophole!"

The commissioner agreed, but obviously could do nothing about it. The law was intended to protect people from exploitation by charlatans and con men, but because it is ridiculously easy to become an "accredited minister of religion" in California, the loophole of Section 43.31 merely serves to push the charlatans and con men into a position where they can *more easily* prey on the weak and the spiritually insecure—and they are immune from the law that was designed to prevent them from doing just that!

(And how easy it is to become an "accredited minister" in California. On April 3, 1972, I read in the Miami *Herald* that a Los

Angeles bar owner, whose liquor license was revoked, reopened his place as a "church." He changed the name of his establishment from the Hi-Life Bar to the Hi-Life Social Club Church, styled himself the "ancient highest head of the church" and went back into business. Instead of selling beer, he gave it away, allowing the members of his "congregation" to make "voluntary contributions" to his "church." All this was entirely legal—he could not be touched by the law!)

"Do you mean," I asked the commissioner, "that if I start my own religion—call it the 'Dykshoorn Church' and myself the 'High Priest'—I can practice as a clairvoyant in California, but not otherwise?"

"That's it," the commissioner said. He was embarrassed about it, and he had gone to some trouble on our behalf to find out if there was any place in California in which I could practice without starting my own "religion," but there was none.

I was amazed at first, then amused. Here I had spent twenty years telling people that ESP is not associated with religion, that we should keep them entirely separate, and the first thing I learned in America was that I should become a "priest." It was so ironic I had to laugh.

Cora was angry, though. She wanted me to work right then and there, in the Century Plaza, for one of our friends, then demand that the commissioner arrest me and prosecute me under Section 43.30.

"We can get evidence from all over the world that Rien *is* psychic!" she said. "We can prove that he *can* tell the future and has done it hundreds of times. The law prohibits *professing* to tell the future, but what if someone can actually *do* it?"

But in the end we decided to laugh it off. We hadn't come to America to fight in court against a law that was patently ridiculous, and if we couldn't live in California without abandoning everything we believed in, we would live somewhere else.

Besides, we had to go to Durham to see Dr. Rhine.

15

THE RHINE RATIONALE: INTENT AND REALITY

We telephoned Dr. Rhine from Pasadena on April 24. He welcomed us to America and invited us to visit the institute anytime. With our plans to look for a home in California disrupted, we decided to settle arrangements with Dr. Rhine before looking elsewhere, so we flew from California to North Carolina on the twenty-seventh and telephoned Dr. Rhine from Raleigh.

He said that he was a little tied up that day but could spare us fifteen minutes of his time.

I was under the impression that he meant he could spare us only fifteen minutes that day, but when we met he quickly made it clear that fifteen minutes were all he could spare for a long time. Testing, he said, could not begin for more than a month.

When I told Dr. Rhine that I had sold everything in Australia and brought my family halfway around the world specifically to submit to his tests, and that I thought at least we could settle arrangements for the testing program, he replied that the institute's schedule was so crowded that he could not fit me into the testing schedule any sooner.

Naturally, I was disappointed. Dr. Rhine had known for months that we were coming to America, and our arrival date. We had telephoned him from Pasadena and again from Raleigh and I had also written to him on April 21. At that time Dr. Rhine must have had his schedule planned, but it was not until we walked into his office in Durham that he told us testing could not begin before the end of May.

I was quite disturbed with this reception, and I was unprepared for some of the other things that came out of our first meeting. Dr. Rhine mentioned several other well-known psychics by name, calling them "frauds and phonies," though he admitted that he had had no occasion to test their abilities.

But the most disturbing thing was Dr. Rhine's apparent unwillingness to discuss any specific plans for a testing program along the lines he had suggested in his letters. I tried to show him my documentation relating to cases in which I had found the bodies and other objects, but he gave it no more than a cursory glance. He seemed to prefer to discuss such subjects as psychokinesis (the ability to influence physical events by means of psychic power), telepathy, and hypnosis—none of which are among my abilities.

This development brought immediate misgivings. "I don't do psychokinesis," I said. "And I'm not a telepathist or a hypnotist. I relate psychically to other people to learn about their pasts, presents, and futures, and I can find things by psychic divining. These are abilities I can demonstrate at any time, but I'm afraid it will be useless to test me along other lines."

In reply, Dr. Rhine produced from his desk a thin pack of blue cards, similar to playing cards but with simple symbols—crosses, stars, squares, circles, and waves—on the faces. I had encountered these cards many times before.

He held up one of the cards so that he could see the face but I could not. "Can you tell me which symbol is on this card?" he asked.

"I don't know," I said. "Perhaps I can, but why should I?"

"Just do it," he said.

"Cross," I said.

"You see? You can do it."

"Of course," I said. "But that has nothing to do with finding out what my gift is, or how it works."

"It's one of our methods," Dr. Rhine said.

Emerging from the institute, we were faced with deciding how we would fill the five weeks before the testing could begin. We had to find a place to live in which I would be able to practice my work without becoming involved in any California-style legal complications.

We chose Miami, and traveled down to Florida, expecting to hear from Dr. Rhine in about a month.

Instead, a letter arrived one week later. After discussions with his colleagues, Dr. Rhine had decided it would not be necessary to wait until the end of May before conducting the series of tests he had planned. He further indicated that testing could begin right away.

Having just arrived in Miami, I had to leave Cora and Helga alone there in a motel while I made the eight-hundred-mile trip north to Dr. Rhine's institute.

On my arrival at the institute I was not tested by Dr. Rhine himself, but by one of the research fellows attached to his staff. For eight hours on the first day I was required to identify symbols on cards. Two different symbols were used, squares and circles. The results were recorded. Then other tests of the same general character were introduced, all involving inanimate objects, and I was told that I would be required to attempt psychokinesis.

I cannot describe the disappointment I experienced. I had come from the other side of the world voluntarily to submit my abilities to tests at the institute, fully expecting that my abilities would be tested according to their nature and according to the use I had been able to make of them over more than twenty years. But these tests were, in my opinion, rather inconsequential when matched against the more substantive nature of my psychic gift.

On the second day I made some suggestions of my own, reminding the staff that from the beginning of our correspondence Dr. Rhine had proposed moving his research in the direction of the application of ESP to human affairs. I suggested that I should be tested with blood samples, as I had been in Europe. This, too, was an unsatisfactory test, but at least it related to living people rather than lifeless objects. My gift, I said, was above all a *human* faculty which related to *people,* and to drive home my point I told some of the staff a few things about themselves—details from the past and present that I learned through my gift.

But my suggestion about the blood samples was rejected. Apparently it did not fit the established research methods of the institute.

Then I suggested that Dr. Rhine should personally accompany me while I worked on an actual murder case in North Carolina.

"If you will make arrangements with the police," I said, "I will conduct a psychic investigation of any case of their choosing while you observe. If the police choose the case and tell me nothing about it in advance, and you are there to witness what I do, there can be no possibility of deception on my part and I can show you how my gift actually works in relation to real, living people."

To my astonishment, Dr. Rhine declined. Instead he suggested that the staff should construct a special murder case situation in the laboratory. They would playact a murder for me to investigate.

I objected to such an arrangement on the ground that my gift takes me into real situations. I emphasized that I experience things that other people have experienced. Situations can't be "constructed" or playacted. Again I suggested that my psychic abilities should be put to the test of working on a true-life murder investigation.

Dr. Rhine refused, indicating that it was not feasible to move outside the institute to witness real psychic phenomena. The testing of my abilities would have to be confined to inanimate objects. He even considered not pertinent the demonstration of psychic knowledge I had given members of his own research staff, even though these people admitted I had told them things about themselves I could not possibly have learned by any means other than through a psychic gift!

That evening Cora informed me over the telephone that a story in the Miami *Herald* had brought people requesting personal consultations. Real people involved in real situations, with real problems on their minds and real questions to ask.

The next morning at the institute, the testing with cards resumed. When I asked how long they were likely to continue playing guessing games, I was told: about a month!

I left for Miami the same evening.

Even then I tried to leave the door open for progress. I was enormously disappointed with the whole situation, because for a long time I had believed that if anyone was going to achieve a really significant breakthrough in parapsychology, it would be Dr. Rhine, who had so much at his disposal in the way of facilities and expert staff.

I was hopeful that a working relationship with Dr. Rhine could be reestablished, and these sentiments were reinforced when I received a letter from one of the research fellows who had tested me indicating that they had found the preliminary results of the tests quite encouraging, and inviting me to complete the tests at some future time when I felt conditions were better.

Perhaps, I thought, we had passed over the first hurdle, and once we started testing my abilities as they were instead of as the researchers thought they should have been, we could make some real progress.

Accordingly, in July we decided to move back to North Carolina in order to be closer to Durham. I wrote Dr. Rhine on the tenth:

> I personally look forward very much to the tests and hope
> we can arrange something in the future, but at the moment
> I have to get some ground under my feet. I now live not
> too far away, so I can easily cover the distance by car.

Although I was aware that my relationship with Dr. Rhine had been damaged by our disagreement, I was unprepared for his reply to my letter. It implied broadly that I had been receiving direct financial assistance or sponsorship from some outside person, which was not the case. Expressing the opinion that things had worked out for me "just like a fairy tale," Dr. Rhine went on to say he could see no need for further testing of my abilities at the institute—especially since it would involve the time and expense of travel!

Only two months before, Dr. Rhine had asked me to leave my family in a motel in Florida and travel to Durham on short notice to undergo testing for a full month. Now, suddenly, the 150 miles between Charlotte and Durham were prohibitively expensive—although I had already offered to cover the distance by car.

Moreover, if the research fellow who had actually tested me had found the preliminary results encouraging, as he had written, why had Dr. Rhine seen fit to overturn that opinion?

The formal end to our relationship was not long in coming, although as it turned out it was caused by a rather trivial incident.

We had settled in Charlotte, and in July a story about me in the Charlotte *Focus* carried the following passage:

> Under the "rose-by-any-name" philosophy, it matters not what Dykshoorn is called, but it is of great import to know what he does. As to the "how" of what he does, even the Dutchman himself does not fully understand that.
>
> But he is one of the few psychics in the country today who is dedicated to aiding scientific research in parapsychology in any way that he can, and shortly after arriving in this country, spent two days at the Foundation for Research on the Nature of Man in Chapel Hill doing card-evaluation tests for Dr. J. B. Rhine. In September, he has volunteered to go back to the lab for whatever further tests the famed pioneer in psychic research might desire to conduct.
>
> This interest in furthering scientifically acceptable information about the subject where other psychics usually prefer to shroud themselves with the mystique of the occult, points

up but one of the ways in which Dykshoorn is vastly different from others claiming similar talents.

Dr. Rhine's reaction to the appearance of this article was swift,
sharp, and final. Although the opinions expressed were those of the
writer, and although it was common knowledge in Charlotte and
Durham that I had been tested at the institute, Dr. Rhine claimed
without warrant that I was somehow responsible for the article
naming the foundation—and he was severing our relationship.

I want to make it clear that I do not object to Dr. Rhine's research methods in themselves. Dr. Rhine has gone on record many
times to say that he feels the primary responsibility of his work
is to establish the "universality" of psychic ability by mass testing,
and he has been largely responsible for spreading the belief that
all people possess extrasensory perception to some degree. In
doing this he has proved that abilities of the mind exist that have
never been recognized by scientists or doctors in other fields, and
he has given parapsychology itself a tremendous boost. I would
not denigrate these achievements for a moment.

However, I feel strongly that confining an analysis of my psychic
talents to statistical tests involving cards or other inanimate objects was hardly an adequate determinant. The ability to identify
cards may signify that a person possesses ESP, but there are or
should be many other criteria—criteria with more convincing
weight—to establish or confirm such powers.

Really, the only thing we know for certain about ESP is that
we don't know very much about it. Certainly we have not reached
the stage where we can *define* ESP, or say that there is only one
test or type of test that can be used to determine whether or not
a person is psychic. Parapsychologists who follow these methods
have proved that certain people are able to identify cards at a
high rate of success, and because they could not have done so using
their five normal senses, they must have done so by using ESP,
or the nonobvious power they call *Psi*. This is fine, this is true—

but actually they have proved only that ESP may sometimes *include* the ability to identify cards, or that this is one *type* of ESP.

I can only wish that Dr. Rhine could have continued our scientific relationship and perhaps gone on to other forms of tests that could have been linked to people and real-life situations in which they find themselves. Dr. Rhine may very well use additional and more wide-ranging testing procedures, but, if so, I was not involved in such procedures.

After all, who is to say that a person who cannot identify cards is not psychic? That person might be able to do fantastic things in other areas. Similarly, a person who can score very highly in statistical tests with cards might not possess any other psychic abilities at all.

I have found human bodies and solved police cases. I solved many cases over long-distance telephone wires. I can also use my gift to tell anyone about his or her past, present, and future, and I can do it at any time, under any conditions. As it happens, I can also identify cards consistently enough to be judged psychic according to the tests devised by parapsychologists, but it gives me no satisfaction to be recognized as genuine by such standards. The ability to identify cards is a very minor aspect of my psychic gift.

The problem is that parapsychology is not a science. In science we look for cause-and-effect relationships and try to discover regularities, and we use the regularities as a law to give a stimulus to get a response.

But in what I do, there are no regularities. Every case is different. There is still a cause-and-effect relationship, because it works and in every case it can be seen to work, but there are no regularities and my work cannot be measured statistically. And because there are no regularities, we cannot give a stimulus to get a response.

When I work with my psychic abilities—when, for example, I find a body—the scientists say this is a *phenomenon* and they can't study it. I consider this a scientific cop-out. Every case in the psychic field is a phenomenon. This is what ESP is all about —psychic phenomena. To ignore phenomena simply because they are phenomena and there are no regularities is to ignore the very crux of the problem.

Some scientists state that what I do is based on superstition, but it is not. In superstition there is no cause-and-effect relationship. There is cause, but no effect. We say that if a black cat crosses your path, you will have bad luck, but it is not so. There is no effect resulting from the cause.

But in my work there is a cause-and-effect relationship, because what I do leads to factual, identifiable results. The basic scientific principles still apply. That is the difference between ESP and superstition; ESP works and can be seen to work, and there is no getting away from the facts.

It is true that most people who are psychically gifted refuse to submit to scientific testing of their abilities, and parapsychologists are inclined to say that these people are afraid of being exposed as fakes. This may be the case with some of them, but it could also be that many of them do not want to expose themselves to such narrow definitions of ESP. A genuine psychic, who can do remarkable work in the human area, may not be able to identify cards at all. As a result, some parapsychologists would be prepared to say that this person is a fraud, which would simply not be true.

This is the great danger of an overly scientific approach to ESP: It ignores the fact that ESP is above all a *human* faculty, and it ignores the potentially valuable psychic phenomena that occur in the realm of human activity. In addition to this, it attempts to place a narrow definition on something we are not in a position to define at all. It is trying to come up with answers when we don't even know the questions.

16

THE CLAIRVOYANT OF
CHARLOTTE, N.C.

When we first moved to Charlotte, several people told us that I would never make it as a clairvoyant in the South unless I hung my gift on religion. This, they said, was "southern bible-belt" country and, generally speaking, the only psychics to gain any popularity were those who attributed their abilities directly to God.

They told me the churches would never accept me if I left God out of it. I told them I don't put God out of it, but only to one side. I believe in God, and therefore I believe that ultimately my abilities come from Him, but only in the sense that all things and all our other human faculties come from Him. I keep my religious beliefs entirely separate from my work and my views on ESP.

I went on television and tried to explain my position with regard to religion—and the next day I had invitations to lecture at Roman Catholic, Methodist, and Baptist churches. And while we lived in Charlotte I lectured to church groups of practically every denomination in the state—as well, of course, to all kinds of nonreligious audiences.

We lived in Charlotte for thirteen months and loved it there.

We finally moved to Miami only because Cora developed an allergy to certain trees which could only be relieved by moving away from the region. Even now I go back there regularly to visit our friends and work for my southern clients.

As in Europe, people came to me from all walks of life for personal consultations, and I worked on all kinds of fascinating problems.

On May 2, 1971, Dottie Smith of Chapel Hill, North Carolina, telephoned me in Charlotte about a lost dog. Her mother, who lived in Charlotte, had just telephoned her to tell her that the family dog, Prince, had been missing since morning.

I worked it out and had to laugh when I learned how Prince had spent his day. In short, he had found a princess in a pen a few blocks away from home and had stayed there all day, outside the pen, his natural instincts thwarted.

"But don't worry," I said. "He will come home either late tonight or early tomorrow morning, and he is all right."

The information I passed along to Dottie Smith proved to be completely accurate and she later confirmed the fact in a letter to me.

One of the problems of working on clients' personal lives is that almost everyone hopes or expects to be told that he or she is going to live an exceptional life, and of course few people do. I can only tell what I see through my gift; if I were to tell all the people who come to me that their dreams are going to work out just right, then I would be no more than a "fortune-teller" and I would have gone out of business long ago. The truth is that only a few of us ever realize our dreams and ambitions. The rest of us change, compromise, settle for perhaps a little less than we had hoped, and live out our lives according to our destinies.

The problem is that few of us like to be told how things will be if they are not going to be as we hope, and this is why I much prefer to work on business problems, or in situations involving practical matters. I hate to disappoint people, but I can only tell what I see as a clairvoyant, nothing more.

Every now and then, however, I encounter a person who is going to live an exceptional life, and who at the time he comes to me is not even remotely aware of what the future holds. I met and worked for such a man while we were living in Charlotte.

Joseph di Bruno came to me for a consultation in February, 1971, and as soon as I started working him out I knew that he was going to be more than a little surprised by what I was going to tell him, because I could see that within a very short time Joseph di Bruno's life was going to change in ways beyond anything he could imagine. And it did.

Like so many others among my clients, Joseph di Bruno kindly agreed to tell the story of my work for him in the form of a legally binding affidavit. This is his testimony:

I, Joseph di Bruno, of 107 Lee Drive, Belmont, North Carolina, wish to make the following declaration, believing that all statements made herein are true and correct:

I consulted with Mr. Marinus Bernardus Dykshoorn, clairvoyant, in February, 1971 at his address in Charlotte, N.C. I had read of him in a newspaper and had been invited to meet him by a mutual acquaintance. Mr. Dykshoorn had never met me before, nor, to the best of my knowledge, had he ever met any member of my immediate family.

During our interview Mr. Dykshoorn revealed to me many details concerning my physical health, family and educational background and life as a child that I do not believe he could possibly have learned by any conventional means of research or investigation.

He stated the nature of my business very exactly. I was a consultant with an oil distribution company with a national franchise.

But Mr. Dykshoorn astonished me by stating categorically and emphatically that within one year of our interview I would be a wealthy man by any standards, and further that in my lifetime I would become involved in international business and finance at the highest possible level, and in fact that my decisions would affect the economies of nations.

Specifically he also stated that I would become involved

with the work of the United Nations in the area of food and nutrition, helping starving people around the world.

Mr. Dykshoorn said that I had worked in the food industry before, which was correct. He said that I had been involved with a chain of hamburger restaurants, but that I had not been an owner in this business. These statements were also correct.

He said that within three months I would meet a man from a national and international food distribution company who would be the cause of my re-entering the food industry. This took place in May of 1971. I was appointed to head a new subsidiary of this company, the only product of which was a highly nutritional liquid substitute for milk.

Within a very short time this new company became so successful that we have now acquired the parent company. My personal holdings of stock in this new corporation are such that I believe I could be described as wealthy by most standards.

The milk-substitute product is such that it is regarded as a significant discovery which may lead to relief for millions of starving people around the world. The United Nations and the World Health Organization have taken a keen interest in it.

At our original interview Mr. Dykshoorn made the remarkable prediction that within six months I would travel to a Central American country as a guest of that country's President, and that this President would express genuine interest in my company's product out of concern for the feeding of his people, and that I would settle a deal for the manufacture of my product in that Central American country before returning to the United States.

Within the specified time I found myself invited to Costa Rica as a personal guest of the President, and a business arrangement was settled while I was there.

I should further add that Mr. Dykshoorn had impersonated the President's manner of walking and that I was able to recognize it.

Mr. Dykshoorn also predicted that within a very short time after our interview I would buy a motel in a sub-tropical area near the sea. This took place although I had not considered it at the time.

Amazingly enough, Mr. Dykshoorn also said that within ninety days I would have cartilage trouble with my left knee, but that during my stay in the Central American country my knee would "pop" back into place and I would have no more trouble with it. All these things have taken place in exactly the circumstances Mr. Dykshoorn described.

Mr. Dykshoorn, in addition to the predictions he made concerning my life and work, also made predictions concerning my son (three years old at the time of writing), which were just as bold and remarkable as those he made for me.

The purpose of these affidavits and other documents is to provide a weight of reliable, irrefutable proof that my gift really does enable me to tell the future with great accuracy, because this is one vitally important area that is being ignored by most parapsychologists. Because it takes months or even years for a prediction about an event in the life of another person to be realized, it is obviously impossible to stage these phenomena under laboratory conditions. But this does not mean that this ability can be ignored, or that recognition does not occur. It does occur. I believe Joseph di Bruno's affidavit is ample proof of that.

I worked on business and technical problems as well. For a Greensboro textile manufacturing company and a hosiery company in Asheboro I did psychic evaluation of product design just as I had for the Dutch shoe manufacturers, indicating which designs would be most successful with which consumer groups.

For a candy manufacturing company I compared wrappers for chocolate bars. As always, I relied entirely on the reactions of my gift and my psychic impressions. They gave me plain candy wrappers in different colors, and asked me which wrapper would catch the eye of a child about nine years old. When I concentrated on the problem, I became like a little child. Not any particular child, but just a child that age—and a little girl, at that. I felt I was a little girl nine years old. Then I went over the wrappers with the divining rod, and it reacted to one of them. I said: "This is the best color."

Then they asked me to go over the designs for the wrappers, and I worked it out the same way. It must have looked very strange to the executives, a grown man behaving like a little girl, but they asked me to do it for every type of candy in their range —and those are the wrappers you will see in the stores.

Once an electrical appliance company in Charlotte asked me to look into some pilfering of materials from their plant. I told them how the materials were being smuggled out, where they were being disposed of in town, and how they were being used. The security staff plugged the holes in their system and the pilfering stopped.

I remember an amusing interlude that took place while I was visiting that company's offices. The staff was out to lunch, and the manager asked if I could tell who worked at each desk. I said I couldn't name names, but I would try to impersonate each person in turn.

The first person I concentrated upon was his secretary. I told him: "Listen, you'd better not fire this woman. She can make life very difficult for you."

"Oh?" he said. "How is that?"

"Well," I said, "she is your wife, isn't she?" And she was.

I also became quite well known among the staff of an airline office in Charlotte. I told a young woman who worked there that within a few months she would be married and living in Africa.

"Africa!" she laughed. "I'm sorry, Mister Dykshoorn, but there's no one I want to marry at the moment, and I'm certainly not planning to go to Africa!"

"Well, don't worry about it," I said. "It will happen anyway."

A couple of weeks later she met a young pilot. They were married on short notice because the young man had to take a flying assignment and he wanted to take her with him—to Africa.

The people of the South were wonderful clients, but they were even more wonderful audiences for my lectures. During the year we lived in Charlotte I lectured to schools and colleges, church and denominational groups, businessmen's associations, women's groups, sporting clubs, societies of people interested in ESP, and even to special-interest groups such as the North Carolina Society of Radiologic Technologists. And everywhere I was pleasantly surprised and flattered by the reception I was given.

At Wingate College, in Wingate, North Carolina, where I lectured on December 3, 1970, Academic Dean Jerry L. Surratt asked me to lecture twice, once in the morning and once in the afternoon, so that as many students as possible could attend.

In the morning only about one hundred students turned up for the lecture. But in the afternoon, after word had spread, more than four hundred students and faculty crammed into the auditorium. Several classes were canceled because both students and teachers, having heard about my morning lecture, wanted to see and hear for themselves.

The purpose and format of my lecture–demonstrations remained the same, with the emphasis on demonstrating my abilities rather than talking about them and with the demonstrations being intended to show people how my gift enables me to know about their lives, and about the lives of people who are, have been, or will be involved with them.

Generally, if a man asks me a question, I will tell him about himself, his parents, and perhaps grandparents, his own wife and family, his job and his home and what will happen to him in the future, as well as answering the specific question he has asked. I do this to show that the answer I give is based on a real psychic knowledge of his life and situation, and not on guesswork or hocus-pocus.

I always try to keep these demonstrations lighthearted, and of course I will never embarrass or make a fool of anyone in front of an audience. The purpose is to show people how it goes, that's all. Inevitably, however, situations arise in which I feel obliged to take a direct hand and offer psychic advice from the lecture platform.

For example, during a lecture I gave to the East Gate Lodge

Number 692 AF & AM (Ancient and Free and Accepted Mason),
in Charlotte, as I worked for a man who had asked me a question,
I learned that his wife was quite ill.

"Sir," I said, "I'm sorry, but your wife is in some pain. Please
tell her to see a doctor."

"My wife is ill?" he replied. "She hasn't mentioned anything to
me."

"I'm sorry," I said, "but I see it. She is suffering from painful
glands. Please ask her about it."

The same man, incidentally, had asked me whether he and his
wife would have children. I told him that they would.

I heard no more about it until I had the following letter from
Leighton H. Moore, master of the East Gate Lodge:

> . . . Brother —— inquired of his wife about the painful
> glands you had asked him about. She acknowledged the
> discomfort she was experiencing but could not understand
> how he knew about it since she had not complained about
> it in his presence.
>
> Also, you informed him that the desired pregnancy would
> come, even though two prior years of trying had failed.
> Mrs. —— is now pregnant.

Who can explain it? I am not a telepathist. I do not read the
mind of the person standing in front of me. I concentrated on the
man, and then on his wife, who was not present at the lecture.
I had the psychic impression that she was ill, and I knew what
her ailment was. But the man who was there at the lecture did
not know a thing about it. He had to go away and ask his wife
to find out that what I had told him about her was true. And
then my gift told me, correctly, that a pregnancy would occur,
even though it was against the odds.

This lecture, incidentally, had some personal significance for me.
I am always pleased when I can lecture to lodge groups, because
I myself have been a Freemason for many years. I have attained

32nd Degree in the Scottish Rite and Knight Templar in the York Rite, and I am a Shrine Ambassador.

On February 4, 1971, I lectured to the College Union of the Belmont Abbey, Sacred Heart College in Belmont, North Carolina. The Belmont Abbey Committee had in mind a shopping-center complex to be built on abbey land, and had submitted two blueprints for council approval. Both had been rejected, then resubmitted. During my lecture they asked me to predict which of the plans would be accepted. The plan I picked was the one eventually approved and built.

Three weeks later, on February 25, 1971, I lectured to the Asheboro Rotary Club. At the end of the demonstration the mayor of Asheboro, Mr. Robert Reece, asked whether I "saw anything happening up on Purgatory Mountain."

This question was not specific enough for me to reply with a specific answer, so I asked what it was he wanted to know. "I see a lot of things happening up on the mountain," I said.

Finally another man stood up. "Mister Dykshoorn," he asked, "do you see Purgatory Mountain being selected as the site of the new state zoo?"

I took up the divining rod and worked it out. "It is between Asheboro and two other towns, is that right?"

"Yes. Concord and Raleigh."

"I am sure that Asheboro will get it," I said.

And Asheboro did, although it had been considered an outside chance.

In June, 1971, I lectured to the 37th Annual Convention of the Carolinas Assocation of Mutual Insurance Agents in Charleston, South Carolina. I was hired to lecture only to the women— the agents' wives—250 of whom were expected to attend.

By this time, however, I had become so well known in that part of the world that I was interviewed on radio and television and the Charleston *Evening Post* carried a long feature on my past work in the edition that appeared the night before the lecture.

The following morning more than six hundred men and women crowded into the hall, and when the demonstration was over—more than two hours later—I was treated to two standing ovations.

It was one of the proudest moments of my life. I felt that I was finally starting to get my message across.

17

MIAMI AND THE "DEVIL'S TRIANGLE"

When eventually we found ourselves obliged by Cora's allergy to move from North Carolina, Miami was the logical place for us to go. We had stayed there briefly while waiting for Dr. Rhine and had liked the climate and the people and, in addition to this, while we were there I had worked on a fascinating case.

This was the mystery of the "Devil's Triangle"—one of the most baffling unsolved mysteries of the world.

The Devil's Triangle, or the Bermuda Triangle as it is sometimes called, is a vast area of the Atlantic Ocean to the east of the southern United States. Its boundaries are indistinct. Some claim it consists of that roughly triangular area contained within lines drawn from Bermuda to Miami, Miami to Puerto Rico, and Puerto Rico back to Bermuda; others state that it is contained within the roughly squarish area between Bermuda, the Coast of Virginia, the islands of Cuba and Hispaniola, and Puerto Rico.

Opinions vary, but whatever its dimensions, some very strange and baffling events have taken place in the Triangle. Depending on the geographical area attributed to it, between one thousand and two thousand people, along with boats and ships and literally dozens of aircraft, have disappeared in the Triangle—just vanished from the face of the earth, without warning and without trace.

The many cases of such disappearance are similar: no debris, no bodies, no flotsam, no oil slicks, no extreme weather disturbances, and no obvious physical disaster.

In March, 1918, a Navy coaling ship, the USS *Cyclops*, with a crew of 309, disappeared without trace. In January, 1948, a British airliner disappeared near Bermuda with a crew of six and twenty-one passengers. The six-hundred-foot tanker *Sulphur Queen* vanished in the Straits of Florida in March, 1963, without leaving so much as an oil slick, which should have been inevitable if the ship had sunk or met with a collision.

Also in 1963 a DC-3 airliner en route from San Juan to Miami vanished within sight of the Florida coast. Literally hundreds of individuals and parties in small boats have also vanished without trace in the broader area, and in no case could the disappearance be readily or even credibly attributed to weather conditions, mechanical or navigational failure, or such "conventional" disasters as fires, explosions, or collisions.

The most astonishing disappearances, however, and those which really brought the Triangle to the notice of the world, took place in December, 1945.

On December 3 a whole squadron of U.S. Navy torpedo bombers—five Grumman TBF Avengers with a total crew of fourteen —took off from Fort Lauderdale Naval Air Station (now Hollywood–Fort Lauderdale International Airport) on a routine training mission. Their flight plan was to take them into the area now known as the Devil's Triangle.

The mission proceeded uneventfully until well into the afternoon. Then at 3:45 P.M., as they were returning to base, the pilots suddenly radioed a frantic Mayday call: "We are lost . . . we cannot see land . . . we seem to be off course . . . we can't be sure just where we are . . . don't know which way is west . . . can't be sure of any direction . . . even the ocean doesn't look right . . . everything is wrong . . . strange. . . ."

In Florida the stunned tower operators tried desperately to get more information on the whereabouts of the squadron or to find out what was happening out there, but radio contact was intermittent and mostly incoherent. Then at 4:25 P.M. one of the pilots was heard to say: "We are not sure where we are . . . we think we must be 225 miles northeast of base . . . it looks like we are entering white water . . . we're completely lost. . . ."

Then there was silence, and none of the pilots or nine other crew members was ever heard from again.

A mariner flying-boat, loaded with rescue equipment and a crew of thirteen, was sent out to search for the missing squadron. That airplane also vanished.

The disappearances launched the most massive sea-and-coastline search ever organized until that time: 242 planes, 18 sea vessels, and an aircraft carrier with 35 more planes covered an area of more than 280,000 square miles in an exhaustive week-long search for some trace—*any* trace—of the 6 aircraft and 27 crewmen who had vanished. Land parties scoured hundreds of miles of coastline in Florida and the Bahamas for any flotsam or wreckage. Even the Everglades and the Gulf of Mexico were covered in the exacting hunt for some clue.

But nothing—not a stick or a stain—was ever found.

A naval board of enquiry could return no definite finding. "We're not even able to make a good guess as to what happened," one board member said. His thoughts were echoed by a Coast Guard spokesman, who said: "We don't know what the hell is going on out there!"

In May of 1970, while we were staying in a motel in Miami, we were contacted by Richard Winer, a documentary film-maker from Fort Lauderdale. He had read about me in the Miami *Herald,* and he asked me to investigate the Devil's Triangle mystery and contribute my ideas on it to a film.

Naturally I was fascinated by the case, and in late May and early June I spent a total of about seven hours working on it in our motel room, in Richard Winer's house in Fort Lauderdale, and at the site of the old Navy buildings, now a junior high school, which had been the barracks of the ill-fated flyers back in 1945.

Incidentally, I made a specific prediction for the film-makers themselves. Richard Winer and his film editor, Ronald Sinclair, remarked that they hoped to persuade Vincent Price to narrate the film, but that they weren't very optimistic about their chances of getting him.

I said: "Oh, you will get him. He is perfect for the job and he likes the story. Don't worry about it, he will do it."

And he did. Ronald Sinclair wrote to me: "You were right about Vincent Price doing the narrative for *The Devil's Triangle.* We recorded his voice for the film last month."

When the final version of the film appeared on television, I was on screen for only forty-five seconds, and most of that time was devoted to my prediction that the inexplicable disappearances will continue to happen. Not that I was worried about it; it was an excellent film and I have no quarrel with the film-makers, who obviously had the right to include or leave out whatever they liked.

Since it was shown, however, I have been asked many times by mail and telephone and in person to explain what I learned about the mystery. Among others, relatives of some of the people who have disappeared have asked me to tell what psychic impressions I had about the Devil's Triangle.

I worked on the mystery as I work on murder cases, concentrating on the victims and experiencing what they experienced in their last moments. I concentrated on each of the pilots of the missing Grumman squadron, the known officers of the USS *Cyclops* and the *Sulphur Queen*, and the pilots of some of the missing airliners.

In each case, my psychic impressions were the same. I felt a tremendous, crushing pressure on my body, as though all the air was being forced or sucked out of my lungs. I could not breathe and I could not move; it was as if I was completely paralyzed by this feeling of enormous pressure. And I saw instruments going crazily awry, needles spinning wildly and uselessly around the dials and gauges. I heard radio static and garbled words and under the enormous pressure everything seemed to blur into a greenish-white mist. I can't describe this, but it may have been a hallucination brought on by the feeling of tremendous pressure on my brain and lungs.

Of one thing I became certain: Each of the people on whom I concentrated died as a result of this crushing pressure. I know that many theories have been advanced for this mystery, among them that the boats and ships and planes were suddenly transported into another "dimension," where the people survived, but I don't believe that. I can only tell of my psychic impressions about the case, and these gave me the idea that the people died.

Also, in each case I had the impression that the sea itself opened up into a huge crevasse, or trough, as though suddenly ripped open by some incredibly powerful elemental force, and that each vessel or plane was sucked down into the sea, which closed over it.

And this, I believe, is the explanation: In two large, ocean-bound areas of the world—in the Devil's Triangle and in another area east of Japan—tremendously powerful magnetic fields are created at various times of the year, usually between December and March, by the earth's own corrections to what we call True North. These magnetic fields are created by the earth itself, and whenever an airplane or ship enters one of these fields at that time, it is acted upon by the magnetism. Its metal parts, which are subject to magnetism, are drawn straight down toward the magnetic center of the earth. The reason there has been no wreckage is that this magnetic force is incredibly powerful—more powerful than anything we can imagine—and everything is drawn deeply into the ocean bed.

This is what I learned from my psychic impressions of the case. I may be wrong and I don't know that it can ever be proved, but I believe it. It may be worth noting that one of the Grumman pilots radioed in his last moments: "We seem to be entering white water . . ." and also that in 1927 a Japanese freighter radioed a peculiar message moments before vanishing forever.

That message was: "Help! Come quick! Like a dagger in the water . . ." But this freighter was not lost in the Devil's Triangle in the Atlantic or the Caribbean. It disappeared in an area of the Pacific between Japan and the Philippines—an area in which an unusually high number of ships and airplanes vanish without trace. Japanese and Filipino sailors call it the "Devil's Sea."

I am often asked if I can foresee death, either of a client or of someone close to a client. The answer is yes. But only under very special circumstances will I say anything about it. Of course, I will never tell a person that he or she is going to die, and the only time I will ever hint that someone else is going to die is when I am absolutely certain that it is right for the person to know.

I believe in predestination, and I am convinced that if I have a definite psychic impression that something will happen, it will happen and cannot be avoided. Neither I nor any of the people involved can intervene to prevent its occurrence. If I see that a person will have an automobile accident, for example, then he will have it even if he resolves never to drive again. One day he will get the urge to drive, and then it will happen.

Accordingly, because I believe this, I have to exercise my own judgment in deciding what to tell and what to withhold—and very often I am forced to withhold a great deal because there is nothing to be gained from the telling. Very obviously, I cannot tell a person he or she is going to die. I could not inflict that knowledge on anyone, and besides, what if I were wrong? I would be responsible for a great deal of unnecessary pain and anguish.

Occasionally, however, I will hint to a person that someone close to him is going to die, but only, as I said, if I am absolutely certain that something of benefit will result from it.

For example, a very good friend of ours in Miami came to me for advice in November, 1971. He was Alex S. Marchando, and he told me he was planning to visit his ninety-one-year-old mother in Youngstown, Ohio, for Thanksgiving.

"Alex," I said, "go at Christmas instead. Your mother would like to have you there at Christmas with the rest of the family, and you know she will live only a week or ten days after Christmas."

Alex changed his plans and visited his mother at Christmas with the rest of his family. She passed away just before midnight on January 3, 1972.

In this case I felt that Alex wanted to know, and had a right to know, and I think that his foreknowledge helped him make his mother's last Christmas a happy one. (See Appendix.)

Captain John H. Goeb, the owner of Ship & Shoe Electrical Services in Miami, came to me in September, 1971, and again I felt that he wanted and deserved to know how things that were distressing him would work out. He volunteered an affidavit on my behalf, so I will let him tell his own story.

On or about September 21, 1971, I consulted Mr. Dykshoorn in his capacity as a clairvoyant on matters of grave importance to me. At that time my business was virtually dead and I was about to succumb to a job offer from a Miami company, at a substantial salary. Also, I was deeply concerned about my late wife's health.

Mr. Dykshoorn not only described my place of origin but also my type of work, without ever having seen me before. He advised me that my business would take a sudden upturn, and not to take a job with any company lest I stood to lose my standing in my field and the clientele I had built up over the years.

Pertaining to my wife, Mr. Dykshoorn sadly informed me that she would not live another year, but that her end would be swift, either by suffering a stroke or a heart attack. He also accurately described my daughter living in New York, and what kind of work she does.

True to his predictions, early in December my business began to pick up and now I am swamped with work. Also, six days before Christmas, my wife suffered a stroke. She passed away on December 22, 1971. . . .

> I can only say that Mr. Dykshoorn does possess genuine powers of extrasensory perception, as has been proved by the fact that his predictions thus far have come true to the letter. (See Appendix.)

Only once that I can remember have I tried to intervene to prevent something happening that I had seen through my gift. In mid-1971 in Charlotte, a woman told me her son had entered an air race. I told her that she must try to talk him out of it. "Tell him he must not go in it," I said. But I knew that he would and be killed. I knew that when his mother told him I had said he must drop out of the race, he would laugh and he would enter anyway.

It all happened. The woman told her son not to enter, but he laughed. He entered the race, crashed and was killed. Perhaps I should never have tried to intervene. I knew that it was the boy's destiny that he die in that crash, but I hated to see it. I believe in predestination, and I believe it was in my destiny that I should learn about it beforehand, and in the woman's that she should learn about it from me.

I am only human, and very often I wish things could be changed, but don't believe they can.

On a more cheerful front, the following affidavit from one of by Miami clients speaks for itself:

> I, Donald H. Roberts, of 1170 NE 100 Street, Miami Shores, Florida, do hereby declare that the following is, to the best of my knowledge, a true and binding statement:
> In October of 1971 I consulted with Mr. Marinus Dykshoorn at his home. Mr. Dykshoorn revealed to me a wealth of detail about my life, work, family, past history and health. I had never met Mr. Dykshoorn before. Moreover, I do not believe he could have gained such personal and private information from any of my friends or anyone else known to me.
> I myself was not aware of some of the facts he revealed to me, and was able to verify them only through research of my own. Specifically, he told me that my mother had

carried two children before me. I had known that a sister born before me had died after four days. My parents are deceased, but my aunt has recently confirmed to me that my mother miscarried on one other occasion.

Mr. Dykshoorn also imitated, in walk and mannerisms, several people known to me but not known to him as far as I know. One of these people I had not met at the time but met later under the exact circumstances predicted by Mr. Dykshoorn.

At the time of my first meeting with Mr. Dykshoorn I was self-employed as a real-estate and mortgage broker in Miami. Mr. Dykshoorn made the following predictions concerning my work and career:

1. Within a year I would accept a job in the same field of activity with a large, diversified company.
2. He predicted an exact salary, that I would be employed as a Vice-President of this company, and would be involved in "building islands," as he put it.
3. He predicted that acceptance of this new position would result in my moving from the Miami area, specifically to the West Coast of Florida.

At the time I had no plans to seek employment, nor any intention to leave Miami. Within weeks, however, I was offered a position as Vice-President of a diversified development company, at exactly the salary predicted by Mr. Dykshoorn, and I accepted.

A major aspect of my activity is the development of waterfront subdivisions, some of them on islands along the West Coast of Florida.

I consulted with Mr. Dykshoorn a second time, November 20, 1971.

On this occasion he predicted that a business deal with which I was involved would be closed before December 31, 1971. He described the people with whom this deal would be settled, and correctly stated that I had already met with them twice. He stated the figure of their first offer for our property ($200,000), and our counter-offer ($220,000), then he predicted that the net proceeds from the transaction would be $200,000.

The deal was closed with the people concerned on the last business day of 1971, with a net to our interests of almost exactly $200,000. At the time I consulted with Mr. Dykshoorn I did not believe that any deal on this property could be closed so quickly.

In other matters Mr. Dykshoorn predicted that I would sell the house I owned in Miami Shores and move to the West Coast of Florida, and he indicated the net price of this house. In early April of 1972 I did sell this house, and the net price was within $400 of the figure Mr. Dykshoorn had predicted in thousands.

He also described to me a home he predicted I would buy on the Gulf Coast. He described in graphic detail the hallway, balcony, stone exterior, entrance and size of lot (more than one acre, he said).

I have not yet bought such a house, but at this time I am considering buying a house which appears to fit the description given by Mr. Dykshoorn. The size of the lot is 1¼ acres.

Don Roberts prepared this affidavit for us while we were living in Miami in 1972. He has since bought the house on the Gulf Coast.

I never make public predictions, especially about the lives of other people. I never work for anyone who doesn't ask me to, I try to mind my own business, and I stay out of the lives of movie stars, celebrities, and royalty. I also stay out of politics and world affairs. I'm afraid I feel that the whole field of ESP has been brought into disrepute by the dismal failure of some so-called "psychics" to predict public events with any degree of accuracy, and I also feel that it is an undignified liberty for any clairvoyant to cash in on sensational publicity by poking his nose into the private lives of celebrities. I have never sought publicity for its own sake, and I sincerely hope I have always avoided "sensational" publicity.

Generally I am kept more than busy with my lecturing, the work I do for my clients, and the important cases on which I work from time to time with the police and other authorities. This is enough for me and I hope the documents we have reprinted so far—along with others set out in the back of this book—will give readers some idea of the kind of work I do.

For my clients I work on their special, individual problems as I worked for Ian Hay in Australia, Joseph di Bruno in Charlotte, and Donald Roberts in Miami. In my lectures I try to convey to my audiences that a strong psychic ability can—in solid reality and not in the realm of fantasy, mystery, and hocus-pocus—enable a person like myself to look deeply into the lives of other people.

On the evening of March 17, 1971, I gave a lecture–demonstration to a group from Epsilon Tau Lambda, an honorary fraternity of adult students and former students from the University of Miami. About a week later I received the following letter from Mr. George Lennox, treasurer of the fraternity:

> Dear Mr. Dykshoorn,
> I wish to express my appreciation for your appearance before our society on Friday evening, March 17. The presentation made by you was beyond our imaginations and almost impossible to believe.
> Our society is an honorary fraternity of adult members who are or have been students at the University of Miami. As such, its members are above the average in intelligence and education. You could not have known any of the members as it is not listed and no public membership roster exists. I make these statements in advance, prior to stating our impressions.
> You were asked questions by various members of the audience. The answers given by you coincided with the knowledge of those who asked you the questions, and even more.
> If you had just told what was in the mind of the questioner, we could have pictured you as a telepathist with the ability to read the minds of the questioners. You did more than this. I cite the following example.
> —— and his wife had just arrived in Miami on the day of the meeting. Mrs. —— asked you a question as to children. Your reply covered the fact of her miscarriages, that she was considering adopting two children, a boy and a girl,

that her husband was working on his doctorate, that they were looking for a house, and that they would not return to Miami.

As a matter of fact, he taught at the University of Miami until last year. He is now working on his Ph.D. at the University of Florida, in Tallahassee. His wife had looked at twins, a boy and a girl, the night before with a view to adoption. He had been looking at houses without the knowledge of his wife. These statements by you bordered on the miraculous as some of the things were not known to each other or to their closest friends.

Other replies by you were equally impressive and unequivocal. There was no possibility of misunderstanding your statements. They were not ambiguous. Our members left with the thorough belief that they had watched a demonstration by a true clairvoyant.

18

MURDER CASES IN AMERICA

At the time of writing this book I have worked on six murder cases in the United States. For obvious reasons I cannot reveal exactly which cases these were, or where the events took place, or the names of any of the people involved. One or two of the cases are still under investigation, while others are being tried or are under appeal. In any event, in each case I entered into a binding agreement with the police not to disclose the fact or extent of my involvement. Any work I do for the police must remain confidential.

There is, too, another reason for withholding the details of actual cases. When I investigate a murder case I tell the police everything I learn from my psychic impressions and usually, because I become so closely involved, psychically, with the people, I tell much more than the police are ever able to prove.

Even in situations where the police have gathered hard evidence from advice I have given them, there have been psychological aspects they have never been able to prove, simply because they could never be proved without a full confession from the criminal.

And because I want to get across an idea of just how deeply I can go into these cases, it is better if we disguise the actual events.

However, it is important to point out that fully documented and legally binding evidence of my work in these cases does exist. While we were living in Charlotte, we became close friends with James G. Bolton and his family, and Jim has accompanied me on each of my murder case investigations in America, acting as an impartial witness and recorder of events.

As I stressed in one of my fruitless letters to the Australian police, one of my purposes in working on criminal cases—apart from the obvious purpose of helping to solve the crimes—is to provide data for study by responsible parapsychologists, so that they might get an idea of what happens during the psychic reconstruction of past events. It was for this purpose, then, that after each of my investigations Jim Bolton prepared an extremely comprehensive and detailed report of everything he witnessed, and has had each statement notarized and dated.

These eyewitness-report affidavits are kept in a safety deposit box, and some day we hope to be able to make them available for proper study. In the meantime, we have to be content with extracting from them and switching the details around from case to case to disguise and protect the people involved. The point, however, is that every incident is based on fact, adapted from fact, supported by legally binding documentation and, above all, real and true.

As far as it is possible to do so, I function the same way in all murder cases in which my assistance is solicited. I prefer to know little or nothing about a case before I start so that my mind remains clear for the psychic impressions. I do not want or need to know the names of the people involved, or any information the police may already have in their possession. I rely entirely on my gift to take me into the situation so that I can reconstruct events as I see them.

I like to visit the scene of the crime, if it is known. There I concentrate first on the victims to find out what happened to them. Then I concentrate on the killers until I have learned all I can about events leading up to and immediately following the killings. Then, by psychic divining, I follow wherever the killers went from the scene of the crime. Wherever they went, I go, and wherever they stopped, I stop. In many cases, both here and in Europe, this has resulted in my finding material clues including weapons, automobiles, and pieces of clothing, and invariably it leads to a place where the killer lives or is well known.

Once I have reconstructed the physical events, I allow the police to ask me questions about any and all aspects of the case—the killers' lives and personalities, their plans and motives and psychological problems, their relationships with the victims and other people in their lives. I also impersonate the people, noting any physical peculiarities and describing them as best I can.

In each instance I provide the police with a comprehensive theory about the case, including as many details as possible, which they can then relate to reality. So far, in every case in which I have been involved some of the information I have turned up has been proved correct, and people have been convicted who matched exactly the people I described from my psychic impressions.

The first investigation in which I participated concerned a double murder in a house in the country. As usually happens, I was called in by the police after they had reached an impasse in their own investigation by conventional methods.

In the sheriff's office I explained that I would go back in time, experience the emotions and feelings of the victims, reconstruct the crime and then follow the killer or killers wherever they had gone afterward. The sheriff asked if I wanted to review the file of the case. I refused and informed him that I would work it out for myself at the scene of the crime. Then he and two detectives in plain clothes took Jim Bolton and me to the house.

It was completely empty of furniture. The murders had been committed several months before, and everything had been removed since then.

I concentrated on the first victim, and immediately felt the familiar sensation of physical change as my psychic identification with the other person took hold. I had the distinct impression that I knew where each item of furniture had been in the house—in the living room, the kitchen, the bedrooms. I described it to the officers: "There was a table here and a chair, and something square, perhaps a small table or a wooden box. Here was the television set, here the bookcase. . . .

"There was a fight," I said. "One of the victims—the woman— was in the bedroom, but there was a fight here between two men. It did not last very long."

Again, as in so many other cases, I experienced the victim's pain, the beating and the blows. The killer had beaten the man and then gone into the bedroom to deal with the woman. As I told this to the sheriff he became quite disturbed.

"We found the woman in the bedroom," he said. "The man was out here. Please go on, Mister Dykshoorn."

"The killer—there was only one, a man—did not force his way in. The victims knew him. He came right up to the door and knocked and the man invited him in. The crime was premeditated. It was not a spur-of-the-moment fight. The man came here to kill the people—no doubt about it. He took the man by surprise and it was a very brief fight."

Then I set out to follow the killer by psychic divining. As I concentrated on him, I started walking differently again. I hunched over, my left shoulder pitching forward, my left arm bending at a strange angle as though deformed. I developed a twitch at the corner of my mouth and could not keep my head from tossing in a nervous jerk. According to Jim Bolton's observations, there also appeared in my face deep lines and creases that are not normally there.

I walked out of the house and plunged into the thick woods

in back of the house where the ground was wet and swampy under-
foot. I seemed to know exactly where I was going, although there
was no definite path through the woods. With Jim and the officers
following close behind, I leaped across a wide ditch I don't think
I could clear under normal circumstances. Later I waded through
a stream and climbed a steep bank on the other side.

For about a mile we strode through the woods, until we emerged
onto a road.

"He hitched a ride," I said. "He was getting tired and he decided
to risk it. He wanted to get as far away from the house as possible. A man picked him up in a truck. The driver knew him.
The killer was very worried when he saw the driver, but there was
nothing he could do about it. I am sure the driver will remember
having picked him up here that day. Later I will give you a description of the driver and his truck and try to tell you where he
lives, but he knows the killer, for sure."

The police sent for a car and when it came we set off again.
I kept the divining rod in my hands and let it guide me. We drove
along the country road for about five miles before I got the reaction
that told me to stop. We were in front of a farmhouse.

"These people know him very well," I said. "This is where the
driver dropped him off. I think perhaps he lives here, or he did at
the time. But he is not the man who owns the farm. Does the
farmer have employees living on the place?"

"He does," the sheriff said.

"That could be it. I will work it out later. Can we go back to
your office now?"

Back in the sheriff's office, the interrogation started. For me this
is always the most fascinating part of a psychic investigation as
the police seek the kind of information on which they build a case.
I never know how much I am going to be able to tell until I am
asked specific questions. Often my gift surprises me by providing
very clear impressions on subjects about which I myself know
virtually nothing—ballistics, for example, or the nature of wounds.

In this case I gained a very clear impression of the murder

weapon. It was a two-foot-long steel bar, hexagonal in shape, with red paint at one end. It was like a stake except that it had no head or point. The killer had concealed it in the leg of his trousers.

The officers agreed that although no such weapon had been found, the victims had been battered to death with a heavy, blunt object and the wounds could have been made by such a club as I had described.

Incidentally, I discovered I was able to identify very closely with the killer. I told the police of his health and family life and what kind of work he did and the fact that he had a distinctive tattoo on one arm.

The questioning went on for hours, then eventually the sheriff asked if I could identify a photograph of the man I had seen in my psychic impressions.

"I don't like to do that," I said. "I don't like to work with photographs or names because I don't like to accuse anyone outright. I can only tell what I see with my gift and you must piece it together in your own fashion. But I will try. Please place the photographs face down on the desk. I don't want to see them."

The sheriff spread five photographs face down on his desk. I took up the divining rod and again concentrated on the man I had seen in the woods. Then I passed the loop over each photograph in turn. As it passed over one of them, it suddenly snapped up from the paper.

Suddenly I felt very tired and weary, as though something had been brought to an end. "I think this is the man," I said. "I'm sorry, but you will have to take it from here."

The sheriff picked up the photograph and showed it to the other officers. They all nodded and one of them noted something on a piece of paper.

I still had not seen the picture. "Does the man have a bent left arm—like this?" I asked.

The sheriff said: "Yes, sir."

"He walks like this, with his shoulder hunched forward?"

"Yes, sir."

"And the tattoo?"

"Yes, sir."

"You recognize him?"

"He is a prime suspect. He used to work at the farm we stopped at."

I am always surprised and fascinated by the mistakes killers make in committing their crimes and effecting their escapes. The man in the foregoing case, for example, *hitchhiked* from close to the scene of the crime to his own home, a stupid thing for him to have done, even though he was picked up a mile through the woods from the house.

Most murders of this type, however, are committed by psychopathic killers with no control over their actions. Even though their acts are premeditated and worked out in advance, they are invariably committed in fury and terror. Once the action starts, the killer has no control over what happens. He stops thinking rationally and very often he can barely remember what he has done. He reacts emotionally, and usually he heads for some place where he will feel emotionally secure again—his home or a location where he will find friends.

Because of this deep emotional involvement, psychopathic murders are easier for me to work out than crimes committed in cold blood, where the killing is only incidental to the purpose of the crime. I never investigate killings by members of organized crime, for example, because there is no emotional involvement. Besides, how can you relate psychically to an organization? Strangely enough, the cases that are the most difficult for police to solve— the irrational, spur-of-the-moment outbursts of hatred and violence —are the easiest for me to investigate with my gift.

One case I worked on recently involved a combination of careful planning and unbelievable savagery by a party of killers. It was another case of multiple murder, but a particularly horrible case of murder by ritual. The bodies of the victims had been found in a clearing in the woods on the outskirts of a southern town, still tied and bound, mute witnesses to the inhuman cruelty that had been enacted on them.

As usual, I was not called into the case until months after the events, but I was able to provide some definite, material assistance.

In the clearing I told the police everything that had happened there—how the victims had been abducted and brought blindfolded to this place, bound and subjected to the insane ritual that degenerated into inhuman savagery. It was a grim, sickening experience, and the police agreed that the wounds on the bodies were consistent with what I had described.

Then I set out to "track" the killers, and my gift took me along a narrow path leading deeper into the woods.

After a long time we emerged into another clearing. My gift took me straight across it to the other side where I found, hidden under leaves and dead branches, some objects that had been used in the rituals.

For reasons of confidentiality I cannot describe these objects, but they were definitely material evidence within the framework of the case. They were not weapons. Rather they were talismanic, symbolic objects that enabled police to identify the "black cult" with whom they were dealing.

At this point the officers became very excited. These were the first material clues turned up in the case. I overheard one of the officers say to another: "I want a complete record of everything this man says."

Later, starting from two points, the scene of the killings and the clearing where I had found the objects, I followed the course each of the killers had taken from the woods. At one point we had to go in automobiles. One of the officers drove while I issued directions along roads that took us to houses and places of business in the district.

The trail of one of the killers led up to the place where one of the victims had worked, even though I had not known anything about the victims before I launched my psychic investigation. Now a relationship had been established: the victims were known to the killers, and vice versa. One of the killers had worked with one of the victims. A motive became apparent; we knew why these particular victims had been chosen.

It must be understood that I do not actually solve murder cases. That is, I cannot accuse anyone by name or construct a case that will stand up in court. These things the police must do themselves, and often this takes months or even years, depending upon how careful the killers have been in covering their tracks. It is often very frustrating, for myself as well as for the police, to *know* who the killers are but still be unable to establish their guilt with solid evidence.

In this case, one of the officers already had a theory about the crimes, I had to tell him: "I'm sorry, but I don't see it that way. It could be, but I don't see it. You understand I can only tell what I see as a clairvoyant."

This was, of course, all I could say. I can't get involved in a case in any way except as a clairvoyant. In this case I did find material evidence, and I believe that was a strong contribution.

As already indicated, in the United States I have always been called in after police investigations have bogged down or ground to a halt. In Europe, where I was better known for this kind of work, my aid was frequently sought immediately after the discovery of the crime, and several times I was able to find material clues—including fingerprints—minutes after my arrival. And I was also able to follow closely on the heels of escaping criminals —once I followed a killer to his home and he was arrested before he had even disposed of his weapon.

Yet it doesn't seem to matter whether a long time has elapsed or not, except for the fact that evidence is often destroyed in the interval. I can reconstruct events that took place years in the past, and my psychic abilities function accurately even in greatly changed physical circumstances.

In one case in the United States, for example, I was asked to investigate a murder that had been committed in a house that had since burned to the ground. There was literally nothing left of the house except a few remnants of brick foundations. We could see where the buildings had stood on the ground, but it was impossible to tell how the rooms had been situated.

Yet I worked on the case as I had on the others and was able to reconstruct everything that had taken place in the house before, during, and after the killings. I knew instinctively where the rooms had been located, and where each item of furniture had stood in each room. The police acknowledged that everything I said matched descriptions of the house as it had been.

I told them where the bodies had been found and indicated that they had been moved after death. They had been found together but had actually been killed in different rooms.

Also in this case I learned that one of the killers had been injured in a struggle with one of the victims, and while we were following this man by psychic divining, I suddenly got a reaction from my gift that induced me to stop the car.

We were at the entrance of the parking lot of a small factory. A middle-aged man who might have been the foreman approached us and the officers engaged him in conversation. I don't like to work on police cases in front of anyone but the police themselves, so I slipped the divining rod into my pocket and moved off to one side.

After a few minutes, however, I got the strong feeling that the killer we had been following was known to the foreman. I called Jim Bolton aside and said: "Get the police to ask him about the man with the injured face. I think he worked here. Not now, but then."

Jim whispered to one of the officers and shortly, very casually, the officer mentioned the injured man to the foreman. Did he recall anyone coming to work with such an injury—oh, about three months ago?

"Oh, yes," the foreman said. "That would be ——."

Also in this case I had some success describing a gun. During the interrogation the police asked if I could see the gun that had been used.

I took the divining rod and moved the loop along the edge of the desk until it flicked upward. But I was puzzled.

"It is twenty-three inches long," I said. "Could that be right—a twenty-three-inch gun?"

"Is it a revolver, an automatic, a shotgun, or what?" an officer asked.

"It is not a revolver," I said. "I don't see the . . . chamber. And it is not a shotgun, either. It fires a bullet, not pellets."

An old automatic pistol was brought from the evidence room, but that was not it.

Then I knew. "It is a cut-down rifle," I said.

There is no point in describing all the investigations on which I have worked for the police in the United States. I cannot report the actual cases because they remain *sub judice*. Nevertheless, I do feel it is important that people should know how it goes in these situations because this is one field where psychic abilities can be immensely valuable to the police, to the friends and relatives of victims, and to the community as a whole. I hope that it will remain an important aspect of my work.

19

THE PRESS IN AMERICA

Publicity, as it inevitably had to do, has played an important part in my life. When you support yourself and your family by providing a service to the public, it has to be that way.

But I have always tried to be careful about the type of publicity I get. I don't seek it for its own sake, I have always tried to avoid publicity of the "sensational" type, and I have never subscribed to the notion that "any publicity is good publicity." I never meddle in the lives of the rich and famous, I stay out of politics and world affairs. Among psychics, too much is done just to attract publicity, and too many tricks and stunts have brought the whole field of ESP into disrepute in the eyes of the public.

I am a working clairvoyant and a lecturer in parapsychology; I try to do my job and let the press say what they will about my work. I stand on my record—that's all. I have had a lot of publicity in my life—in Europe, Australia, and here in the United States—and in this book I have quoted from many newspaper stories, but all of them have resulted from work I have actually done, not from what I believe about myself or things I have said about other people to cash in on their fame.

Clairvoyants, of course, make what newspaper people call "good copy." People are always interested in reading about ESP. My own file of press clippings covers more than twenty-five years of my life, and they do not contain one lie or false statement. Many of them deal with cases on which I used my talents; others are interviews with or profiles of myself written by journalists who have talked with me about my work.

Many others, however, are more than simply stories in which my past work is reported for the informational value. They are, instead, reports of journalists' own personal experiences, of how I worked for them and how I told them things about their own lives which turned out to be true.

I have already quoted from one or two stories of this type in the Australian section of the book, and I would like to quote now from a few that have appeared in the United States.

I would like to do this for a particular reason. Journalists are strange people; almost without exception they are skeptical and suspicious of people like myself who claim to be psychic, and in my experience it is only very rarely that a journalist will personally endorse a clairvoyant's abilities. That several journalists have done so for me here in the United States is a source of great satisfaction to me because, by reporting honestly and objectively on the work I did for them, they have contributed greatly to my main aim in life, which is to promote a deeper and more realistic understanding of ESP and its possibilities.

The following was written by *Kannapolis* (N.C.) *Independent* staff writer Marvin Eury on September 27, 1970:

> . . . [Dykshoorn] can, in an exaggerated way for emphasis, imitate a manner of walk, speech, or appearance of a man or woman he has never met.
>
> These are documented accomplishments, cold facts as recorded and sworn to by those persons with whom Dykshoorn has come into contact.
>
> This reporter met the amazing 50-year-old Dykshoorn last week.

With the aid of a piece of piano wire which spins in a certain way if he is on the right track, he noted this reporter had a slight back-ache. He was right.

Then, although he had never seen this reporter walk except for a step or two, he demonstrated with great accuracy the jaunty, slightly hopping manner of walk that has been an Eury trademark for at least two generations.

With a broad smile he noted that the extra weight on one leg caused the slight ache.

It was but one incident that made the interview with Dykshoorn one of the most unforgettable interviews in a 35-year journalistic career.

Staff writer June Kronholz made the following observations in the Miami *Herald* for August 23, 1971:

"I'm working you out," Dykshoorn says in a heavy Dutch accent, as he studies his whirling divining rod. "I don't tell you what you want to hear; I tell you what my gift sees. I'm just the man in between."

Suddenly he stops pacing, his eyes sparkle under his bushy black eyebrows, he looks up from his divining rod.

"Your father, I can see him—he walks like this, his hands behind his back," says Dykshoorn, imitating the very familiar walk of a very familiar man living 1,600 miles away.

"And I see your brothers, two of them. One is like this," and he imitates the blond's web-footed, bouncing trot and the other's shuffle.

But Dykshoorn doesn't stop there. He looks back at his divining rod, now spinning again, his stocky frame paces the floor and he continues. He tells about operations, college careers, marriages, children, ages, occupations, stitches you never knew your mother had.

"Your mother-in-law is seventy," he'll say. "But what's the matter with her arm?" There's nothing the matter with her arm, Dykshoorn, Ha! Caught you that time!

"Go home and ask her," he says confidently.

And he is right, you learn. She had a stroke once; it paralyzed her arm and left it weak. . . .

And finally in this selection of stories, from Elaine Boies in the Staten Island *Sunday Advance* of March 4, 1973:

> Passing a loop of piano wire over the human skeleton on an anatomical chart, [Dykshoorn] stopped suddenly and told me my husband had a chronic problem with his right ankle. I was embarrassed for him, answered a tentative "Well, maybe," but Dykshoorn insisted.
>
> I tried to be polite, but said I didn't know of any such ailment, and we've been married for seventeen years.
>
> We let it drop then, and the short, stocky man, whose ice-blue eyes gleam from under a thatch of shaggy brows, dropped his right shoulder and walked towards me. "Your husband walks like this," he said.
>
> His imitation was so perfect, it was hilarious. Not a caricature, but the astounding shock of recognition told it like it was.
>
> Later, I told my husband—a skeptic—about meeting Dykshoorn, and swore to him that though the clairvoyant had started out on the wrong foot with the ankle bit, his mimickry was indeed amazing.
>
> My skeptic husband looked thoughtful and said: "You don't know about my ankle, do you?"
>
> Obviously he was putting me on, teasing me for being gullible.
>
> Except that he spent an hour telling me about a lifelong distortion of the foot that causes him to wear down his shoes improperly, suffer pain and throw his whole body out of alignment.
>
> And why hasn't he mentioned it in seventeen years? Because, like any birth defect, it's a "natural" condition he has lived with all his life.

In the United States I have also appeared many times on television and radio. After one appearance on WB-TV in Charlotte, Ty Boyd, who interviewed me on the air, wrote:

> What a sensation to have you on our Noon Report television show. Our switchboard was busy with calls, our viewers eager for more. Thank you for coming. . . . you are indeed a most fascinating man.

Then after another appearance on television in Charlotte, Milton Bagby of WSOC-TV was moved to write:

> Your comments were thought provoking and we received a number of responses to your being with us. As you know, I am highly skeptical of the mystical, the seer, the fortune-teller and some clairvoyants. I say some clairvoyants, for I believe you are an exceptional man with a great gift.
>
> In particular, I am struck with your insistence that you should not be called a minister or holy man. I recently saw on television another clairvoyant whose predictions and visions were made entirely in a Christian framework. I wonder how a Moslem or a Hindu would accept what she has to say! I appreciate your honesty. . . . Please visit with us again.

20

A PERSONAL CONCLUSION

In this book I have tried to describe some of the cases on which I have worked as a clairvoyant, to provide enough documentation to prove beyond reasonable doubt that the things I have described really did happen, to convey some of my personal feelings about the field of parapsychology and to give you some idea of what it is like to be a clairvoyant in this world.

I have not tried to describe all my cases, or to include all the documentation I have in my files after more than twenty-five years as a practical parapsychologist. To do this would require a book of a thousand pages; it is enough to say that only a small proportion of my work is reported here, because I wanted only to give the reader some idea of how it goes.

If I have taken issue with some scientists in the field of parapsychology, I would like to make it clear that it is only with *some* scientists that I disagree, and then only with some of their methods of research. No scientist has ever tried to harm me in my work, and some have been very helpful to me, especially in Europe and the United States.

My concern is for parapsychology and it is for this reason that I have learned to express myself in terms of psychology and scientific principles. It is important to me in my interpretation of the things I see, hear, feel, taste, and smell through my psychic abilities.

However, my gift is still a personal thing. It can't be learned. Every case is different and needs a different approach. For my own part, I never know which approach to take on a case until I start on it. Then it comes to me. This is why I use the term "instinctive" to describe my abilities. In *The Scientific Principles of Psychology* (1963), by Donald J. Lewis, professor of psychology at Rutgers, the State University of New Jersey, the term "instinct" is defined as "*a long-continuing, complicated, co-ordinated unlearned pattern of behavior,*" and this is the closest term I can find to describe my gift as far as I know it.

You can't learn it. "Learning" is defined as "*a relatively permanent change in behavior as a result of practice [trials].*" I don't believe that any amount of trial or practice will result in anyone learning to do what I do as a psychic.

In my work there is a cause-and-effect relationship, the basic principle of science, but we have never been able to discover the regularities that we can use as a law to give a stimulus and get a response. It is my opinion that parapsychology can never be an exact science, for just as every case is different, I believe that every psychic person is different.

Nor does it have anything to do with education. I have met illiterate people who were very good psychics, even though they could not express themselves well enough to communicate with people in terminology that could be understood.

Since our arrival in the United States I have met many openminded and dedicated scientists and they have helped me learn the proper terminology with which to express myself. In return I have invited them to accompany me on cases of parapsychological interest, to observe my work as I do it and to question me about my psychic impressions. I have been very pleased with the way they have accepted me as a practical parapsychologist and their concern for the human aspects of ESP. I hope that by working in cooperation we can come to a better understanding of this difficult and complex subject.

In conclusion, I would like to ask the reader once again to make his or her own judgment on the material in this book. It goes against much of what has been written in the past about the subject of ESP and psychic phenomena, but it is factual and one thing I have learned in my life is that you can't fight facts.

APPENDIX

The following affidavits testify to the accuracy of predictions made by M. B. Dykshoorn.

To-day,the eleventh of October nineteen hundred and forty nine,at half past one p.m.,I,Robert Batten,Notary Public,station Middelburg,was in the house Seisstraat 28 at Middelburg,in the presence of the witnesses to be mentioned hereafter,where appeared before me:

Mr.Marinus Bernardus Dijkshoorn,dowser,residing at Breda, Wilhelminasingel 7a.,born at 's-Gravenhage,the tenth of July nineteen hundred and twenty and known to me,Notary Public,according to his declaration acting in this matter as oral mandatary of Mr.Anton Gerard Touburg,pensioner,residing at Maassluis,Fenakolinslaan 31.

The appearer declared:

that in said house lived Mr.Jan Hendrik Meijboom,who from there evacuated to.Lisse,where he died on the seventh of December nineteen hundred and forty eight; he did not leave behind wife or relations in the direct line and by his last will, passed before the Notary Public H.R.Struve at Middelburg,of the nineteenth of November nineteen hundred and twenty eight,he indicated his sister,Mrs.Johanna Pieternella Meijboom,as his sole heiress,the latter being married to said Mr.Touburg,in entire community of property;

that,according to the communication of his principal, said Mr.Meijboom,before being evacuated from Middelburg,should have buried an amount in silver coins in the garden of said house,which coins,as far as his principal knows,were never found;

that said Mr.Touburg therefore instructed the appearer,to look for this buried sum of money with the dowsing-rod,at the time and at the place as aforesaid.

The appearer therefore requested me to draw up an official report of the looking for these coins.

Complying with said request I was in the kitchen of the aforesaid house,with the appearer and the witnesses,where the appearer,before beginning with the dowsing,gave a description of the person of Mr.Meijboom,which came up to the reality. Thereupon the appearer went with the dowsing-rod into the garden of aforesaid house and indicated a place under the back-kitchen where the money should be buried.After digging there,they found there,unpacked in the loose earth,total three hundred silver rixdollars,so total an amount of seven hundred and fifty guilders

Of which this official report has been drawn up in minute, ah the time and at the place as said above,all this in the presence of Willem Pieter van Aartsen,lemonade-manufacturer and Janis Marinus Lakerveld,clerk,both residing at Middelburg,as witnesses.

Immediately after reading this deed,signed by the appearer,the witnesses and by me,Notary Public

M.B.Dijkshoorn, W.P.van Aartsen,J.M.Lakerveld,

R.Batten,Notary Public.

Issued as a copy

For true translation:

PH. FICKINGER
GEDIPLOMEERD
GERAAR HANDELSCORRESPONDENT
EN TOLK
BEEDIGD VERTALER
ENGELS — Nederlands — DUITS
POTER BUK 119 - TEL 7796 . BREDA

The declaration by Notary Public Robert Batten of Middleburg, testifying that in 1949 Rien Dykshoorn was able to find a cache of silver coins that had been buried in the garden of a house in Middleburg since the Second World War.

SHIP & SHORE
Electrical Services

P. O. Box 1411

Miami, Florida 33138
February 4, 1972

Subject: Testimonial
Re: Mr. Marinus Dykshoorn
To: Whom It May Concern

On or about Sept. 21, 1971 I consulted Mr. Dykshoorn in his capacity as a clairvoyant on matters of grave importance to me. At that
time my own business was virtually dead, and I was about to succumb
to a job offer made to me by a Miami company, at a substantial salary. Also, I was deeply concerned about my late wife's health.

Mr. Dykshoorn not only described my my place of origin but also my
type of work, without ever having met me before. He advised me that
my business would take a sudden upturn, and not to take a job with
any company, lest I stood to lose my standing in my field and the
clientele I build up over the past years.

Pertaining to my wife, Mr. Dykshoorn sadly informed me that she would
not live another year, but that her end would be swift, either by
suffering a stroke or a heart attack. He also accurately described my
daughter living in New York, and what kind of work she does.

True to his predictions, early in December my business began to pick
up and now I am swamped with work. Also, six days before Christmas,
my wife suffered a stroke and passed away on Dec. 22, 1971.

A close friend and business associate of mine who visited Mr. Dykshoorn independently and without my introduction, also benefitted
from Mr. Dykshoorn's predictions, in both his business matters and
in his domestic life.

I can only say that Mr. Dykshoorn does posess genuine powers of
extra-sensory perception, as has been proven by the fact that his
predictions thus far have come true to the letter.

Signed,

Capt. JOHN H. GOEB
Owner, Ship & Shore
Electrical Services

acknowledged before
me 2/17/72
                    10-26-74

AFFIDAVIT

STATE OF FLORIDA)
) ss
COUNTY OF DADE)

BEFORE ME, the undersigned authority, personally appeared MARVIN H. GILLMAN, who after being duly sworn, under oath does depose and say:

I am MARVIN H. GILLMAN, a practicing attorney in Miami, Florida. In April, 1972 Mr. M. B. Dykshoorn, who had consulted me for legal advice, stated to me in response to my query of what the result of a pending case before the United States Fifth Circuit Court of Appeals would be, that my client would be victorious in the matter, that the Appeal I had taken would be successful in spite of the fact that all persons connected with the matter, except the undersigned, were pessimistic of its outcome. The case had then been pending before the Court of Appeals for almost five (5) months after oral argument. In October, 1972 I was advised by the Court of Appeals that the Appeal had been successful by a unanimous opinion. The written opinion encompassed twenty six (26) pages and was a change of previous existing case law that had been relied upon by my adversary and by the lower court, United States District Court for the Southern Jurisdiction of Florida.

In October, 1972 Mr. Dykshoorn stated to me that I would be awarded a substantial fee by the court for my services

212

in the matter. In September, 1973 the lower court awarded a fee of $48,000.00 for my services in the matter.

More amazing than his accurate prediction of the outcome of the particular case was his description to me of my client's physical appearance and the physical appearance of the three Appellate Court Judges who heard the case. These descriptions were without any assistance whatsoever by me and without revealing the names of the client or the judges, none of whom, to my knowledge, has he ever seen pictures of or met.

FURTHER AFFIANT SAYETH NOT.

Marvin H. Gillman
MARVIN H. GILLMAN

SWORN TO AND SUBSCRIBED BEFORE ME,
this 6th day of March, 1974:

Catherine Leigh Tyndall
NOTARY PUBLIC, State of Florida

My Commission Expires: NOTARY PUBLIC STATE OF FLORIDA at LARGE
MY COMMISSION EXPIRES DECEMBER 16, 1977
BONDED THRU GENERAL INSURANCE UNDERWRITERS.

December 20, 1970

Dear Mr. Dykshoorn,

In 6 days, we will have been here 2 months and feel like this is really where we belong.

If you will recall, on August 6th you told me that the lease from my apartment would be broken and we would be leaving Charlotte shortly.

September 1, we were evicted and left Charlotte on October 24th.

You also predicted that 3 girls would take over the apartment and they would be nurses. You have been absolutely right.

The day I moved, I saw the maintenance man and he told me 3 girls were moving into my apartment and I asked him were they nurses? And he said he didn't know for sure, but they worked at Charlotte Memorial Hospital. I wrote to a neighbor and asked her to find out what those girls are and the reply came yesterday - Nurses.

I was waiting for the reply before I wrote to you as I had to be sure. You also told me that the man who has my father's money is in the hotel business.

I met my father's lawyer today wo is vacationing down here and when I mentioned this to him, he replied "That's right, he's got interests in a hotel".

I thought the enclosed article may be of interest to you, since you told me the story of "The Devil's Triangle."

Wish you could get vibrations from this letter and tell me what's coming next.

It sure softened the blow when I got evicted to know that this was supposed to be happening.

Wishing you and your wife a health and happy New Year.

Sincerely,

Shirlee Charatz

Shirlee Charatz

You have my permission to use this letter in your book.

Shirlee Charatz

NOTARY PUBLIC, STATE of FLORIDA at LARGE
MY COMMISSION EXPIRES JULY 26, 1974
BONDED THROUGH FRED W. DIESTELHORST

214

A F F I D A V I T

STATE OF FLORIDA)
)
COUNTY OF DADE   )

Before me this day personally appeared ALEX S. MARCHANDO,
who, being duly sworn, deposes and says that on
November 11, 1971, he consulted with MR. M. B. DYKSHOORN.
MR. MARCHANDO told MR. DYKSHOORN that he planned to visit
his 91-year-old mother in Youngstown, Ohio over the
coming Thanksgiving holidays. MR. DYKSHOORN said it
would be better if you could go over the Christmas holidays;
"You would see more relatives and could have a nice visit
with your mother before she dies, because she will only
live a week to ten days after Christmas."

MR. MARCHANDO changed plans and visited his mother and
many relatives over Christmas. He returned to Miami
December 29th and before midnight January 3, 1972, his
brother telephoned informing him that his mother had just
died.

                 Alex S. Marchando
                 Signature of Person Making Affidavit

Sworn to and subscribed before me this first day of
February, A. D. 1972.

                Montey F. McFarland
               Notary Public
               State of Florida at Large
              NOTARY PUBLIC, STATE OF FLORIDA AT LARGE
              MY COMMISSION EXPIRES JAN. 23, 1973
              BONDED THROUGH FRED W. DIESTELHORST

STATUTORY DECLARATION

I, Jacob Gobes, of 250 George Street, Sydney, ——————————————

—of—————————————————————————————— in the State of New South Wales

————————————do solemnly and sincerely declare as follows:————————

Several years ago I was the proprietor and owner of a
restaurant in Sydney. At this time I met Mr. M.B. Dykshoorn,
who to my surprise told me that my restaurant would be burnt
out not once but twice. I forgot about the prediction until
2½ years later when my business was in fact burnt out. Still
I thought this may have been coincidence, but eight months later
the building was burnt out again.

On another occasion Mr. Dykshoorn visited a restaurant of which
I was the proprietor and told me that the following day the
chair in which he was sitting would be occupied by my first
employer. I doubted this for two reasons: firstly because that
particular place was occupied every day at lunchtime by a regular
customer; secondly because my first job had been at an hotel in
Holland when I was 13 years old and I could not even remember
the name of my employer at the time.

The following day my regular customer brought a guest to
lunch, although he sat in his usual place. Then suddenly the
two men changed places, so that the guest occupied the chair
Mr. Dykshoorn had nominated. I was later introduced to the guest,
who, after learning my name, said he had been the manager of
the hotel in Amsterdam/I had worked there. *when*

Then on another occasion Mr. Dykshoorn warned me against wearing
a particular item of clothing for a special evening, saying that

    And I make this solemn declaration conscientiously believing the same to be true and by
virtue of the provisions of the "Oaths Act of 1900-1953".

Subscribed and declared at *Sydney*
this 28th day of *April*
one thousand nine hundred and
before me

STATUTORY DECLARATION

I, _____

of _____ in the State of New South Wales _____

_____ do solemnly and sincerely declare as follows: _____

misfortune would result if I did. I forgot the prediction and
did wear the item of clothing on the particular evening. Afterwards
I was involved in a serious motor accident and was hospitalised
for a considerable time.

On yet another occasion about five years ago Mr. Dykshoorn told
me that I would work for a large company in a circular building
in Sydney, although at the time I was entirely self-employed and
had no intention of changing that situation. Mr. Dykshoorn further
told me in some detail the nature of the catering work I would
supervise in my future employment.

I now manage a catering business in the circular tower in Sydney
known as the Australia Square Tower. The nature of my work is
almost exactly as Mr. Dykshoorn described. It is remarkable that
at the time Mr. Dykshoorn made his prediction, the Australia
Square project had not been commenced or even announced.

And I make this solemn declaration conscientiously believing the same to be true and by
virtue of the provisions of the "Oaths Act of 1900-1953".

Subscribed and declared at *Sydney*
this *28th* day of *April*
one thousand nine hundred and
before me *W. Wardrop, J.P.*

February 25, 1974

In May of 1970 we experienced what has proven to be one of the outstanding events of our lives.

Three guests checked into our Travelodge Motel in Hallandale, Florida -
namely Mr. & Mrs. Rien Dykshoorn and their daughter Helga. This was the
beginning of not only a lasting friendship but a most exciting knowledge
of Rien's abilities as a clairvoyant. His advice to us and generosity in
sharing his gift, have been most valuable and reassuring.

Our first questions were concerning the future of the motel. He assured
us immediately that it would be sold in the near future and that we would
be pleased with the final settlement. He also said that someone would come
into the office one day before noon and by the same afternoon the sale would
be consummated. His description of timing was the reassuring factor
during several months of delays that were to follow. The sale was completed
as he described last December, in spite of the many intervening difficulties.

Our son was preparing for college entrance at the same time. Rien assured
us he would not only be very pleased in his choice of colleges but would do
quite well academically in a course of study he had not previously considered. This is the field he is pursuing as his Major.

Recently our daughter and son-in-law were planning the purchase of a motel.
Tampa was the prime consideration. Upon consulting Rien, he asked if the
motel was "L" shaped and we agreed that this was true. Later we found it
to be in the shape of a "T". However, he maintained that they would move
to Tampa.

Some time passed before a definite offer was made, only to find it had been
sold. However, the seller owned another in Tampa by the same chain name.
This was "L" shaped. That was also on option and presumed sold by the
owner. It was later discovered the persons holding the option had re-
neged and they were able to purchase the motel last November.

These are only a few of the detailed facts Rien has given to us that
have occurred exactly as he predicted.

Charles Nickens Jr.

Charles Nickens, Jr.

I. R M H Nickens

Mrs. Charles (Irma) Nickens
1001 Washington St.
Hollywood, Florida

Sworn before me this __26__
day of February, 1974.

JoAnn Bryant

Notary

NOTARY PUBLIC, STATE OF FLORIDA AT LARGE
MY COMMISSION EXPIRES NOV. 12, 1976
BONDED THROUGH MUROSKI - HUCKLEBERRY, INC.

SEAL

STATUTORY DECLARATION

I, Enid Seabrook, 57 Chuter Avenue, Ramsgate, N.S.W. 2217

of ———————————————————————————— in the State of New South Wales

do solemnly and sincerely declare as follows:

Here are the predictions you forecast for me which were so accurate it was
unbelievable .
1. At that time you said my marriage would be broken and I would remarry a man
I already knew who would have to do with the sea, would have 3 children and
his wifewould be as fair as my husband and his work would have to do with the
Crown.————— All this would transpire within a period of of 4 years and I would
change my name during the 10th month. Subsequently I did remarry a man I had
known for 10 years with the name Seabrook which brought in the sea and his
business was importing which brought him under the sing of the Crown as most of his
business was involved with Her Majestys customs with the crown over the door.
His previous wife was as blonde as predicted similar to my exhusband and at that
he (my present husband) had 2 children but by the time we were associated, he
had 3 children. Our weddingdate was the 6th October (10 month) before the four
years stipulated by you had exspired. You also predicted I would assist my Husband
with my hands to make money and now I have succesfully started a manufacturing
section in which my hands are in use constantly creating. You also said I would
go overseas (which I did) and I would dislike London (which was true)as I was
quite ill at the time. I might add that the decision to go was quite sudden.
My prior position to my 2^e.marriage was the manageress of a substantial retail
business which you said. I would leave and a male would take over, which did happen
I had been in this position for 12 years and had no intention of leaving.
These are the main issues. Many other small things were predicted (which came true)
but would take many pages to relate. I have been very satisfied and surprised at
the accuracy of the predictions and most certainly hope to consult him during the
coming years if possible. This is a true and accurate statement.

And I make this solemn declaration conscientiously believing the same to be true and by
virtue of the provisions of the "Oaths Act of 1900-1953".

Subscribed and declared at
this   27^e day of April
one thousand nine hundred and sixty nine
before me

E. Seabrook .

STATUTORY DECLARATION

I, LESLIE STANLEY BULLOCK,

of 58 Raglan Street, Manly ——————————————— in the State of New South Wales

————————————— do solemnly and sincerely declare as follows: For the past three months I have been interviewing people who have consulted Mr.R.Dykshoorn, Clairvoyant,and have obtained statutory declarations from some of them.Every one of the people I interviewed,without exception,was amazed at the accuracy with which he described their past and present.In a significant number of cases,predictions had come true within a matter of weeks. When I consulted him personally,I was most impressed with his description of my childrens' personalities,even though he had never seen them and had never heard me talk about them.He described them exactly, and pointed out talents and personality traits that I had never noticed.When I looked at the children later I could see that he was right.He described accurately the way I think and feel about many things.He described the problem which is worrying me most at the moment and pointed out a solution which I am certain is the best one possible.He even told me that my Mother is still alive,is about 80 years old,is in very good health for her age but gets dizzy in the mornings.This is absolutely correct. Such a simple thing to tell yet so amazingly accurate.He had no way of knowing about this.The best description I can give is that he "read me like a book". That is exactly what Mr.Dykshoorn appears to do with everyone who consults him. He is without doubt the most amazing man I have ever met.

And I make this solemn declaration conscientiously believing the same to be true and by virtue of the provisions of the "Oaths Act of 1900-1953".

Subscribed and declared at *Sydney*.
this *Seventh* day of *May*.
one thousand nine hundred and *Sixty nine*
before me

220

Volksbund Deutſche kriegsgräberfürſorge e.V.

DE GEMACHTIGDE VAN DE VOLKSBUND IN NEDERLAND - JOSEF OECHSLE

Herrn

M. B. D ij k s h o o r n

B r e d a
Liesboslaan 156

AMSTERDAM-W
COPPELSTOCKSTRAAT 48¹
TEL. NO. 12 58 93

20. Juli 1954.

Sehr geehrter Herr Dijkshoorn !

Es ist mir ein Bedürfnis, Ihnen mitteilen zu können, dass es
mir gelungen ist, die Grablage der 2 deutschen Soldaten, die
im September 1944 im Albertkanal bei Lanaeken in Belgien er-
trunken und als "unbekannt" begraben waren auf dem Friedhof
für gefallene deutsche Soldaten in Lommel zurückzufinden.

Diese Tatsache stützt sich in der Hauptsache auf Anweisungen,
die Sie mir geben konnten.

Für Ihre Bemühungen möchte ich Ihnen dann auch meinen ganz
besonderen Dank aussprechen.

Mit vorzüglicher Hochachtung !

Josef Oechsle.

Translation of this letter from Herr Josef Aechsle of the German War-Graves Commission reads: "It is my pleasure to inform
you that I have succeeded in finding in Lommel the burial places
of the two German soldiers who in September 1944 were drowned
in the Albertkanal near Lanaeken and were buried as "unknown"
in the cemetery for fallen German soldiers. This resulted directly
from instructions you gave me."

INDEX